WR LLS

MIKE GOULD

 Pearson

 YORK PRESS

The right of Mike Gould to be identified as the Author of this Work has been asserted by him in accordance with the Copyright, Designs and Patents Act 1988

YORK PRESS
322 Old Brompton Road, London SW5 9JH

PEARSON EDUCATION LIMITED
Edinburgh Gate, Harlow,
Essex CM20 2JE, United Kingdom
Associated companies, branches and representatives throughout the world

First published 2017

10 9 8 7 6 5 4 3 2 1

ISBN 978–1–2921–8636–8

Phototypeset by Carnegie Book Production
Printed in Slovakia

Text credit: Extract from 'The Highwayman' by Alfred Noyes reproduced by permission of The Society of Authors as the Literary Representative of the Estate of Alfred Noyes.

Photo credits: Jacob Lund/Shutterstock for page 7 bottom / Tupungato/Shutterstock for page 8 bottom / Rawpixel.com/Shutterstock for page 10 top / Rawpixel.com/Shutterstock for page 10 top / AKaiser/ Shutterstock for page 12 middle / mrmohock/Shutterstock for page 13 middle / Ian Law/Shutterstock for page 17 bottom / Colin_Hunter/© iStock for page 18 bottom / sezer66/© iStock for page 20 top / Matt Gibson/Shutterstock for page 24 middle / Thanawat Pholthanya/Shutterstock for page 29 middle / andriscam/Shutterstock for page 32 bottom / MihailDechev/© iStock for page 36 bottom / scull2/© iStock for page 39 bottom / Chrislophotos/Shutterstock for page 40 top / Andrew Zarivny/Shutterstock for page 40 middle / lisasaadphotography/Shutterstock for page 42 middle / Eky Studios/Shutterstock for page 43 middle / VICUSCHKA/Shutterstock for page 47 bottom / SAHACHATZ/Shutterstock for page 52 bottom / Eriks Z/Shutterstock for page 54 bottom / John A. Anderson/ Shutterstock for page 56 middle / ranplett/© iStock for page 57 middle / Roman Kosolapov/Shutterstock for page 61 top / De Space Studio/Shutterstock for page 65 bottom / natsusora/Shutterstock for page 66 top / mRGB/ Shutterstock for page 69 bottom

CONTENTS

CHAPTER ONE: CORE WRITING SKILLS

CHAPTER TWO: PLANNING, DRAFTING AND CHECKING

CHAPTER THREE: RESPONDING TO TEXTS IN THE EXAM

CHAPTER FOUR: WRITING YOUR OWN TEXTS

CHAPTER FIVE: PUTTING IT INTO PRACTICE

CHAPTER SIX: ANSWERS AND GLOSSARY

1.1 'WRITING' IN BOTH GCSE ENGLISH LANGUAGE AND LITERATURE

Understanding the different types, styles and forms of writing required in your exams is vital to success. You also need to understand *where* and *how* your writing is being assessed.

ENGLISH LANGUAGE ASSESSMENT OBJECTIVES

The two assessment objectives in GCSE English Language upon which your writing will be assessed are:

	• Communicate clearly, effectively and imaginatively, selecting and adapting tone, style and register for different forms, purposes and audiences. • Organise information and ideas, using structural and grammatical features to support coherence and cohesion of texts.
	Use a range of vocabulary and sentence structures for clarity, purpose and effect, with accurate spelling and punctuation.

These AOs are assessed in extended essay-style responses in the 'writing' sections of each exam paper.

ENGLISH LITERATURE ASSESSMENT OBJECTIVES

In GCSE English Literature, the main 'writing' assessment objectives, relating to how well you express ideas are:

	Read, understand and respond to texts. Students should be able to: • maintain a critical style and develop an informed personal response • use textual references, including quotations, to support and illustrate interpretations.
	Use a range of vocabulary and sentence structures for clarity, purpose and effect, with accurate spelling and punctuation.

Bear in mind that even if you are being tested on reading skills (for example in the other half of the English Language paper), you need to show your knowledge through what you write down.

❶ Which two assessment objectives are identical across the two GCSEs? Why do you think this is?

WHAT TYPES OF WRITING WILL I HAVE TO DO?

In **GCSE English Language** these include:

- **Succinct, precise sentences or paragraphs** explaining your understanding of ideas or information provided
- **Longer responses** in which you **summarise points** or information or **compare two texts**
- **Longer responses** where you **explain more complex or detailed ideas** in paragraphs
- **Extended imaginative/fiction response** which might be descriptive or narrative (story-telling)
- **Extended personal non-fiction response** which provides a viewpoint or opinion on a topic

In **GCSE English Literature** these include:

- **Longer responses to extracts** from **Shakespeare plays** and **19th Century novels**
- **Longer responses to essay questions** (not based on extracts) on **modern novels** and **plays**
- **Longer responses to poems** from the **Poetry Anthology** you have studied
- **A 'medium-length' response** to an **unseen poem**
- A slightly **shorter response** to a **second unseen poem** comparing it with the first

As you can see from this, it is vital that you can adapt how you write to the question asked.

Don't

- Write long, rambling answers to questions worth a few marks
- Write short, undeveloped answers to questions which require detailed analysis

Do

- Check the requirements of each task
- Judge how much and what sort of writing is needed

❷ Although this book is mainly about your GCSE English Language and English Literature work, writing is important in all subjects. What other subjects that you study require:
  - short, sharp factual written answers
  - comparison answers
  - long essay-style answers based on source material such as a text or image?

APPLYING YOUR SKILLS

❸ Here are two typical exam-style questions, one from GCSE English Language and the other from GCSE English Literature. For each one, estimate:

- How **much** you might write in response: a few short or medium length sentences; two-three paragraphs; a full-length essay
- How **many marks** out of 30 you think each would be worth (marks for each section are not always out of 30 but it is a useful guide)

A

> Read from **Line 19 to 29** of the extract by the writer in which she describes the prison.
>
> How does she use language in this section to make you feel sympathy for the people inside it?

B

> How does Priestley explore guilt in *An Inspector Calls*?
>
> Write about:
>
> - the ideas about guilt in *An Inspector Calls*
> - how Priestley presents these ideas by the ways in which he writes.

Remember:

- Writing is important in all your exam papers – it's what examiners see!
- However, writing skills are assessed specifically by particular questions.

1.2 TASK, AUDIENCE AND PURPOSE

Matching the **tone** and content of your writing to its purpose and **audience** is an essential skill. It shows that you understand how to use language, and how to create an impact on an audience.

BREAKING DOWN THE TASK

To do this, it is helpful to break down the task. For instance, look closely at the purpose and the marks awarded. What do these tell you? Consider the following example:

> *Needs to include explanation and analysis of writer's methods*

> *Details content of the task: the elements to be covered*

'How does Priestley explore guilt in *An Inspector Calls*?

Write about:

- the ideas about guilt in *An Inspector Calls*
- how Priestley presents these ideas by the ways in which he writes.

(30 marks)

> *Shows the overall focus – across the whole play*

> *For this many marks it must be a well-developed response*

In other questions, in GCSE English Language, the task might be set out more explicitly, with the **form** and **purpose** stated in the wording:

> *Says exactly what type/form of writing you have to use*

'Charity shops have no place on our high street.'
Write an article for a local newspaper in which you argue for or against this point of view.

(30 marks)

> *Reveals the purpose – the reason for writing*

Different purposes

Most texts have a main purpose (such as inform, explain, entertain, describe, narrate, persuade). But writers may use several purposes to achieve the main one. For example, read this:

> *So, we now have several charity shops on our high street; our once tatty main street that until a year ago was full of empty, boarded up buildings suitable only for rats to raise happy families in. In their place, as I walked past today, were treasure troves full of books, clothes and other useful items, where the lonely old lady who lives on our corner can go for a chat, a browse and to pick up a bargain.*

❶ What is the **main** purpose here?

❷ What evidence is there of *other* writing purposes, for example to inform, to describe, to advise, to tell a story?

UNDERSTANDING AUDIENCE

When you see the word 'audience' it usually means 'the reader' or 'readers.' Sometimes the audience will be fairly obvious (even stated in the exam task), or you may have to work it out. For example:

Audience: students; possibly some teachers

Explicit: stated clearly, obvious	*Write the text of a speech for the student council at your school in which you argue for or against the removal of all snack and drinks machines.*
Implicit: needs to be worked out	*'Once a month, there should be a traffic-free weekend in our town/village.' Write a letter to your local newspaper in which you argue for or against this viewpoint.*

Audience: whoever reads the local newspaper – probably mostly adults, but from the area

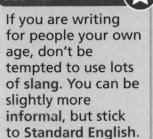

TOP TIP

If you are writing for people your own age, don't be tempted to use lots of **slang**. You can be slightly more **informal**, but stick to **Standard English**.

You will need to match your tone and what you write to the audience.

EXAM FOCUS

Read one student's opening paragraph responding to the first task:

Starts with personal reference

Mentions the intended audience

> I want to talk to you about something important to us all in the school, whether we are students or teachers. Our health. I strongly believe that the school is sending out the wrong message by allowing snack and drinks machines to eat up our money, and at the same time fill us with salt, sugar and harmful chemicals.

Refers to 'us' further emphasises writer is 'one of the group'

❸ How do the writer's language choices in the rest of the paragraph indicate:
- he/she is talking to fellow students
- he/she is making a persuasive speech?

APPLYING YOUR SKILLS

Now read this opening sentence in response to the task about traffic (above):

It is surely the case that the inhabitants of Gorton-by-Sea would welcome a weekend without the encumbrance of traffic in their town.

❹ Continue in the same **formal** style, adding a further sentence or two.

1.3 FORMS OF WRITING

You will be asked to demonstrate your understanding of different forms of writing in your GCSE English Language exam. While you will not have to produce all of these forms, being prepared to tackle them is important. For example, depending on your specific course, you might be asked to demonstrate your knowledge of one or more of the following:

> a speech,　　　letter
> a diary extract　　a blog or email
> a newspaper article or report
> an imaginative description
> an original story

CONVENTIONS

Each of these writing forms has its own **conventions**. These are the particular uses of language, structures and patterns we would typically expect to see in this form of writing.

① Which of the forms of writing in the box above might include the following conventions (there may be more than one)?

A
Written in **third person** (He/She)

Dramatic events or **climax**

Speech as well as descriptive language

B
Written in **first person** (I)

Recounts very recent events

Reveals personal or secret feelings/emotions

C
Written in first person

Likely to focus on topic writer feels strongly about

Probably uses present **tense** (I feel, we are, etc.)

TOP TIP

Conventions are *not* rules. It is quite normal for forms to mix or share conventions – for example, a travel article could contain vivid description, like a story.

VIEWPOINT OR PERSUASIVE WRITING

This is one of the most common types of article you will have to read or write in GCSE English Language. It is often:

- A newspaper or magazine article
- Written by someone who has a particular view on an aspect of life
- Lively and personal (sometimes humorous)

This form of writing is quite similar to personal speech or letter to a newspaper (although the **audience** may be slightly different in some cases).

AIMING HIGH

The best way to learn about the conventions of a particular form is to read examples of it. Newspapers can be useful sources as they include news reports and opinion pieces as well as more literary writing, such as travelogues, reviews, etc.

EXAM FOCUS

Here is the opening to one student's opinion piece.

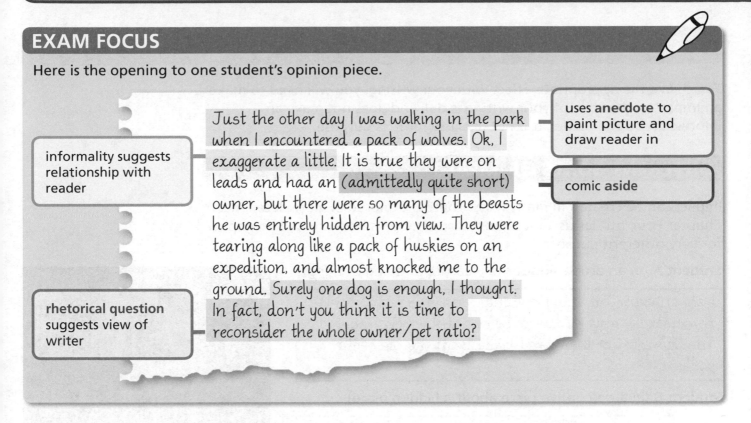

informality suggests relationship with reader

Just the other day I was walking in the park when I encountered a pack of wolves. Ok, I exaggerate a little. It is true they were on leads and had an (admittedly quite short) owner, but there were so many of the beasts he was entirely hidden from view. They were tearing along like a pack of huskies on an expedition, and almost knocked me to the ground. Surely one dog is enough, I thought. In fact, don't you think it is time to reconsider the whole owner/pet ratio?

uses **anecdote** to paint picture and draw reader in

comic **aside**

rhetorical question suggests view of writer

2 What opinion does the writer hold?

3 In this piece, some key conventions are apparent in the opening paragraph. But how (if at all) would this have been written *differently* if it was:

- a story
- a diary entry?

WRITING CRITICALLY

Another key form of writing, not mentioned at the start of this unit, is the 'critical essay'. This is dealt with in Chapter Three, but it is worth pointing out some of its conventions here:

- **Standard English**
- Analytical and clear expression
- Use of quotations or close reference to evidence/information
- Written in paragraphs with a clear conclusion
- Generally uses the present tense
- Avoids using the first person 'I' directly; tends to use 'we', 'the reader' or does not use any of these

4 You will need to write critical essays for both GCSE English Language and English Literature. What other subjects that you study involve critical writing similar to this?

APPLYING YOUR SKILLS (A05)

5 Check the details of your GCSE English Language paper carefully and note down the different forms of writing you will have to demonstrate. Make sure you are clear about:

- Where and when each form of writing is needed
- What common conventions you might use for each

1.4 CREATING AN IMPACT

To achieve the appropriate effect with your writing, you will need to make an impact. If the style of your writing is dull and does not make an impression on the reader, it is not likely to fulfil its purpose.

DIFFERENT SORTS OF IMPACT

Impact can be created in many ways. These is explored in more detail in Chapter Four, but let us look at how three students have created an impact for very different purposes.

Student A (in an article about the pleasure of doing nothing)

> I am an expert in doing nothing. A connoisseur. A genius. A maestro. If anyone was to be awarded a Gold Medal at The Olympics for inaction, I would be at the top of the podium.

Student B (in a descriptive piece about a hidden place)

> Under the curving, falling caresses of a willow tree, lies a sunken pool of limpid water. Like an emerald sheet it ripples ever so slightly in the wind, and the tall reeds bend and sway like nodding soldiers on parade.

Student C (in the opening to a story about an imprisonment)

> Inside the locked door, the room was like a shoe-box, measuring about 3 metres by 2 metres. There was a single, iron bed with a thin mattress, and a painting on the wall of an ice-capped mountain. This, then, was my prison. And all because of a ring.

❶ Impact is about effect. Which of these effects are created by the texts above? Copy and complete the table below to record this information.

Effect	Student A	Student B	Student C
a) Brings to mind a vivid scene or moment			
b) Uses a comical **analogy** to make a point			
c) Impresses by using repetitive patterns, but not in a 'boring' or dull way			
d) Creates shock or sudden impact through short or minor sentences			
e) Creates interest or mystery			
f) Uses **irony** as an undertone			

VARIETY AND SURPRISE

It can also be effective to introduce *change* into your writing. For example:

a) Moving from **long sentences** to **short** ones

b) Having a **single sentence paragraph**

c) Moving from **description** to **action**

d) Moving from description or action to **dialogue** (speech)

e) **Speeding up**, or **slowing down** by careful use of **punctuation**

f) Introducing **humour** (appropriately)

g) Introducing a **serious** point, after something **lighter**

h) Introducing a different, **contrasting character** or **place**

i) **Changing time** – flashing back, or forward, in a story

❷ Which of the above changes are used in the following example from a story?

> *Brother Francis looked at his careworn, lined hand which held the cracked cup of lukewarm tea. The sun beat down on his bald head in the monastery courtyard. He stared into the dregs thoughtfully.*
>
> *'Penny for them, brother?' said a voice.*
>
> *Francis had not noticed his colleague Luis approach.*
>
> *His mind went back to his arrival at the monastery – a young man of 25, pulling up in his sports car, escaping his life as a top flight professional footballer – yes, that is how it had all begun.*

AIMING HIGH

In general, it is better to **show** a scene or setting or a person's actions and movements rather than just to **tell** us how they feel. Look again at the Student C example from the previous page and how specific things are shown to the reader to convey the idea of imprisonment.

APPLYING YOUR SKILLS   (A05) (A06)

❸ Write two paragraphs about two very different people meeting for the first time. Use any of the 'impact' ideas from this unit to create an effect.

Remember:

● Make your writing deliberately surprising or vivid.

● 'Show' what is happening by describing physical objects, actions, people's faces, etc.

TOP TIP

Vary your vocabulary, too – but always with an effect in mind. Note how on page 12 Student A uses three different words which are all **synonyms** of 'expert' ('connoisseur', 'genius', 'maestro'). This adds rhetorical impact to the slightly unusual point being made.

1.5 USING QUOTATIONS EFFECTIVELY

It is essential when you are writing longer responses in your English Literature essays to use quotations effectively. Your points need to be expressed clearly and fluently, and quoting well will help you to do this.

THE BASICS

Remember:

- **Quotations** mean the **actual words** you have taken from the text you are studying.
- Always use **speech marks/inverted commas before** and **after** the quoted words or phrases.
- Only **quote what is necessary** – never long paragraphs of text.

GRAMMATICAL FLUENCY

Read this short passage from the end of *A Christmas Carol* by Charles Dickens:

> *'I don't know what to do!' cried Scrooge, laughing and crying in the same breath; and making a perfect Laocoön of himself with his stockings. 'I am as light as a feather, I am as happy as an angel, I am as merry as a school-boy. I am as giddy as a drunken man. A merry Christmas to every-body! A happy New Year to all the world! Hallo here! Whoop! Hallo!'*

Now read these two student responses:

Student A:

> Scrooge is totally transformed at the end of the book, 1 am as happy as an angel.'

Student B:

> Scrooge is totally transformed at the end of the book, saying that he is 'as happy as an angel.'

Note how in the second, to embed the quotation fluently in the sentence, the student has:

- Shortened the quotation – by removing 'I am'
- **Paraphrased** the missing part by adding a linking **phrase** – 'saying that he is'

This is a more impressive way of expressing your idea, so try to embed quotations where you can.

Now read **Student A's** further point.

> Scrooge goes on to describe 'I am merry as a school boy' and 'giddy as a drunken man'. This further emphasises how joyful he is.

❶ This doesn't quite work grammatically. Can you rewrite it, following the advice above?

TOP TIP

Shortening quotations and paraphrasing can help prevent your writing becoming clumsy.

TOP TIP

Look out for words or phrases which you can quote and link together in your response. For example, 'Scrooge describes himself as "merry", "giddy" and "happy".' The point uses three **adjectives** effectively to stress what we learn about Scrooge.

QUOTATIONS IN PARAGRAPHS

A common structure you may know is: **P** (Point), **E** (Evidence – often the quotation), **E** (Explanation). For example:

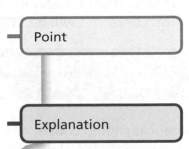

> Romeo believes he is in love with Rosalind He speaks of his love being like 'a smoke raised with the fume of sighs.' This sounds rather exaggerated, not the words of true feeling.

Evidence

Point

Explanation

This is fine, but using this structure all the time makes writing very dull.

Consider this alternative:

> Describing his love as 'a smoke raised with the fume of sighs' at the start of the play, Romeo's exaggerated description of his feelings for Rosalind suggests these are manufactured emotions. In other words, he is in love with the idea of love, not the actual person.

❷ Where is the 'evidence' here?

❸ Has anything further been added to the overall explanation?

SINGLE WORD QUOTATIONS

There is nothing wrong in selecting single words to quote from a text. In fact, doing so may help you focus in on the selected word's potential meaning and interpretation. For example:

Well-chosen single word quotations

Meaningful interpretation of quotations

> When Romeo uses the words 'smoke' and 'fume' to explain his love for Rosalind, the use of these nouns suggest that his thinking is confused and clouded. This can be contrasted with Juliet's 'brightness' in Act 2 Scene 2 which cuts through Romeo's foggy thinking.

In addition, placing similar words together like this can reveal some interesting ideas.

AIMING HIGH

You can show variety in how you present points by developing the 'P.E.E.' structure. For example, you can add a further point at the end – as shown in the example ('P.E.E. plus', if you like), or you can even swap the 'P.E.E.' structure around, for example by beginning with a quotation and then exploring it ('E.P.E.').

TOP TIP

When you make links across the text, use clear **connectives**. For example, you could link between the extract and other parts of *Romeo and Juliet* by writing 'Furthermore, *in* Act 1 …' or '*Later* in the play …'

APPLYING YOUR SKILLS (A01) (A04)

❹ Check your use of quotations in essays you have written so far. Evaluate them according to their clarity, grammatical fluency and variety.

1.6 SPELLING, PUNCTUATION AND GRAMMAR

Accurate use of spelling, punctuation and grammar in your written work is vital. 20% of your marks in GCSE English Language, and up to 5% in GCSE English Literature will be awarded for these aspects.

CHECKING THAT YOUR SENTENCES ARE CORRECT AND EFFECTIVE

Sentences should consist of a **subject** and a **verb** and make sense in terms of the grammatical order of ideas too. For example:

- *Stella* [subject] *called* [verb] *her parents.*   **Correct** ✓
- *Stella her parents.*   **Incorrect** (no verb) ✗
- *Her called Stella parents.*   **Incorrect** (wrong order grammatically) ✗

TOP TIP

Be careful with your subject and verb agreement. For example, 'Stella *don't* like me' is **incorrect**, as the form 'don't' goes with 'I', 'you', they, we'. For 'he' and 'she', it should be '*doesn't*'.

The main **sentence types** to be aware of are:

Sentence type	Definition	Example
Simple sentences	These have a subject (the person or thing who 'does' the action) and main verb and usually (but not always) an object (who 'receives' the action), like the example opposite. They consist of one main **clause** that makes sense on its own.	*Stella called her parents.* subject **verb** object
Compound sentences	These join together two main clauses or simple sentences. These are usually equal in importance. They are linked by **conjunctions** such as 'and', 'so', 'but', and 'or'.	*Lady Macbeth drugged the guards but Macbeth murdered the king.*
Complex or **multi-clause sentences**	These contain a main clause with additional **subordinate clauses** or phrases in support of the main or complete clause.	*The play is a tragedy* (**main clause**) *even though the hero kills the rightful king* (**subordinate or dependent clause**), *who was decent and kind.* (**further sub-clause**).

Minor sentences are short sentences which do not have a main clause, e.g.:

> 'Good morning, Ryan. Why are you late?' said Mr Rudd.
> 'Overslept….'
> 'That's not an excuse, is it?' Mr Rudd went on. He was unimpressed. Angry, too.

Use minor sentences for exclamations, sayings or responses to questions, or for dramatic effect, but bear in mind that they are sometimes not considered as 'proper' sentences so use them sparingly.

AIMING HIGH

Examiners want literature essays to be interesting to read. Think about how changes from longer to shorter sentences can emphasise points or ask questions of the reader.

EXAM FOCUS

Note the use of all three main sentence types in this student's response to *An Inspector Calls*:

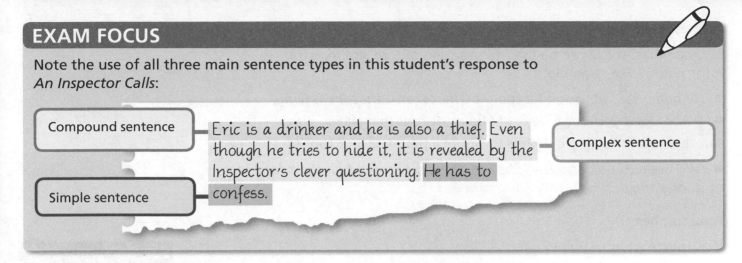

Compound sentence

Simple sentence

Complex sentence

Eric is a drinker and he is also a thief. Even though he tries to hide it, it is revealed by the Inspector's clever questioning. He has to confess.

❶ Write a paragraph about a character from one of the texts you are studying. See if you can imitate the structure of the paragraph above. (You could add a quotation to one of the sentences.)

PUNCTUATION FOR MEANING

It is easy to think that punctuation just means a set of rules to follow, but its main purpose is to indicate tone or mood and clarify ideas. You should already know that all sentences must end with either a full-stop, question mark or exclamation mark. But what about the other main forms of punctuation?

Commas can be used in several ways:

- To **separate items** in a list: 'Jane Eyre follows the path of child, school-girl, governess and wife.'
- To **link adjectives** when more than one describe the same thing: the wild, windy terrain of the moors stretched before her.'
- **After dependent clauses** in sentences: 'Having fled her marriage, Jane felt lost and alone.'
- In pairs **to insert additional information** into a sentence: 'The house, which had been out of view thus far, finally appeared.'

The comma splice

The comma splice is a common mistake where two independent clauses or sentences are split ('spliced') using a comma. For example:

'We roamed the moors, it was wonderful.'

The correct way to write this is to use either:

- two separate sentences:
  'We roamed the moors. It was wonderful.'

or

- a single sentence with the comma replaced by a conjunction:
  'We roamed the moors and it was wonderful.'

Dashes and brackets

Like commas, these can be used to separate out, or slot in extra information. For example:

- *He believes – although he could be mistaken – that she is lying.*
- *He believes (although he could be mistaken) that she is lying.*

Another use for a single dash is to signal a pause or interruption to speech:

- *'We need to talk about—' Shahena began to say, when she heard the door slam.*

Apostrophes

Use apostrophes in two ways:

- For **contractions** – when words are shortened and letters omitted: e.g. 'It's' = 'It is'; 'They're = they are' etc.
- To show **possession** of something: e.g. 'the queen's ambitions', 'Juliet's drink'; 'The two lovers' letters'

TOP TIP

If there is just one 'owner' put the apostrophe in front of the 's'. If there are two or more 'owners' then the apostrophe comes after the 's' (as in 'the two lovers' letters').

Speech punctuation and layout

You are most likely to use speech punctuation in your creative writing but, if you do, you must get it right. Here is a correctly punctuated speech from one student's exam response:

Speech marks at start and end of spoken words; capital letter for first spoken word

New line for new speaker

Punctuation related to what is said, inside final speech mark

Continue on same line if same speaker speaks again

'Get back from the harbour wall!' the man shouted, battling against the wind.

'Why should I?' cried Lisa, tears streaming down her cheeks. 'What's the point?'

Varying 'said'

Your use of speech or **dialogue** will also look and sound more professional if you vary the verb alternatives for 'said'. For example, using 'replied', 'asked', 'cried' 'whispered', 'grumbled', etc.

However, sometimes it can be even more effective to leave out who is speaking and the verb altogether, particularly when two people are talking. For example, see this continuation of the harbour wall dialogue:

> 'There's always a point!' the man called, battling the gale.
>
> 'How would you know?'
>
> 'Because I once stood where you are standing now,' the man continued, climbing the stone steps.

Semi-colons

Use the semi-colon in these ways:

- To **separate items** in a list of phrases rather than single words: e.g. 'the windswept moors; the empty house; the cries from the attic.'
- To **separate two main clauses** instead of a conjunction (and to avoid the comma-splice mistake), e.g. 'The Inspector shocks them all; each family member has to face his or her crime.'

Colons

Use the colon in these ways:

- To **introduce a list**: e.g. 'The signs flashed by: motel, ranch, diner – but no clue where the bank was.'
- To provide a **definition, elaboration or explanation**: e.g. 'We felt a surge of emotion: Verona, sight of the greatest love story of them all.'

❷ Continue the story of Lisa from page 18, writing an additional two paragraphs. Include some further dialogue, varying your use of 'said', and make sure any other punctuation you use is set out correctly.

PUNCTUATION WHEN QUOTING

Remember: you also must always use speech marks or inverted commas when you need to quote the actual words a writer has used in a text you are studying. For example:

The actual words written by Charles Dickens, including full stop within inverted commas

Dickens opens his novel with the words, 'Marley was dead, to begin with.' This curious statement arouses our interest – if he was dead 'to begin with', what has happened to this man now?

Single inverted commas at start and end of quoted words

Shorter fragment of quotation treated in same way but comma outside inverted commas

SPELLING

Correct use of spelling is a vast topic, so what follows are really just a few reminders of the most common errors you might make. Remember, that some of these are to do with usage (i.e. selecting a word which is correctly spelled but used in the wrong situation).

There, their and they're

Misuse of these is one of the most common errors you can make, especially when writing quickly in an exam. Remember:

- 'There' is usually used as an adverb, often but not always referring to place: e.g. 'The wall had broken and there lay Lisa, alive but very shaken.'
- 'Their' is possessive pronoun referring to 'they/them': e.g. 'Their clothes were scattered on the floor.'
- 'They're' is a contraction of 'They are', particularly in more informal speaking or writing: e.g. 'They're on the way over here.'

Also note that:

- 'Where' relates to place (e.g. 'Where are my socks?') but 'wear' is a verb (or noun): e.g. 'I want to wear my new socks'. Neither of these is spelled 'were'!

Confusing contractions

It is easy to confuse words that look or sound the same or use a **contraction**. The key is to be clear about how you use them.

- 'Were' is the past tense of 'are': e.g. 'They are home now, but they were at the market this morning.'
- 'We're' is a contraction of 'we are': e.g. 'We're off to see our cousins.'
- 'Your' is a **homophone** of 'You're': but, 'your' means 'belonging to you' whereas 'you're' is a contraction of 'you are', e.g. 'You're are as clever as your sister.'
- 'Too' and 'to' are easy to mix up. 'To' is generally used as a preposition, e.g. He walked over to the door') or as a part of the infinitive form of a verb ('He went to sleep'). Whereas 'too' means an over-supply or excess amount, e.g. 'He had too much sleep.'
- 'It's' is often used as a contraction of 'It is', using an apostrophe, e.g. 'It's busy on the roads today.' However, 'its' is used without an apostrophe to show something belonging to 'it', e.g. 'The shopping trolley lost one of its wheels.'

Other commonly confused words

- Accept and except: 'accept' is a verb meaning to agree, or to say 'yes' to an offer, e.g. 'She accepted she was wrong.' 'Except' is usually a preposition or conjunction which means 'but not': 'Everyone was invited except me.'
- Affect and effect: 'affect' is generally used as a verb, and 'effect' as a noun, e.g. 'He was affected [verb] by the news…' and 'The effect [noun] of the news on him was striking.'

SPELLING ADVICE

Try the following approaches to improve your spelling.

Specialist words

You can be fairly certain that particular words will crop up in your English Language and Literature exams. For example, it would be extremely unlikely that you would complete the exams without using the word 'character' or 'relationship'. Write out a list of core terms you are likely to use (check over your past essays or revision notes to find them) and make sure you learn their spellings thoroughly.

- character
- relationship
- theme
- location
- scene

Mnemonics

A **mnemonic** is a memory aid which helps you recall troublesome spellings. Popular ones are acrostics, such as '**n**ever **e**at **c**heese, **e**at **s**ausage **s**andwiches **a**nd **r**emain **y**oung' ('necessary'), but you can create your own – for example, breaking words down into parts: 'cha/rac/ter'.

Look, say, cover, write, check

Look carefully at the word you want to spell; **say** it out loud; **cover** it up; **write** it out; **check** to see if you spelled it correctly.

Learn families of spellings

Build up your spelling knowledge of words around the specialist terms you might use by creating spelling families: for example, *narrate; narrative; narrator; narration.*

APPLYING YOUR SKILLS

❸ Draft two paragraphs explaining the impact of an important (but not the main) character in a play or novel you have studied.

- As you work, consider each of the sentence types you are using, and consciously think about your use of punctuation: is it appropriate and does it help the meaning? Check your writing to ensure you have avoided the comma splice!

- Once you have finished, do a line-by-line proof-read, marking up anything you think might be incorrect or unclear. Check against the advice or guidance in this chapter – plus any other spelling rules or conventions you know – and rewrite the text.

PROGRESS CHECK FOR CHAPTER ONE

GOOD PROGRESS

I can:
- Understand the basic skills required of the tasks in GCSE English Language and Literature ☐
- Use some of these skills to make my writing clear and appropriate to the task ☐

EXCELLENT PROGRESS

I can:
- Understand the different writing requirements of each task ☐
- Use these core skills to create impact and/or write analytically ☐

2.1 GENERATING IDEAS

No matter what writing task you have to do, making sure you have good ideas or a range of suitable points to make is vital. But how do you do it?

THE TYPE OF TASK

The type of task and amount of time you have both matter. Typically, you will have about 45–50 minutes for writing tasks in GCSE English Language, but you may have less time for certain GCSE Literature questions. In all cases, it is crucial to get good ideas down on paper quickly.

STARTING WITH THE TASK

Let us take a typical GCSE English Language exam task:

> *'Interest in social media, parents' safety worries, lack of green spaces – there are many things that stop young people living active lives.'*
>
> Write an article for your school magazine in which you persuade fellow students to become more active.

Start by underlining or highlighting the key words from the title. This will focus your attention on the task, and help you to select an appropriate **style** and **tone**. Here, a student has started the process:

> *'Interest in social media, parents' safety worries, lack of green spaces – there are many things that stop young people living active lives.'*
>
> Write an article for your school magazine in which you persuade fellow students to become more active.

❶ Now note down any other key words or phrases (for example, relating to **audience**, **form** of writing, etc.).

WAYS OF GENERATING IDEAS

You could use a **spider diagram**. Note how in this case, the student has used some of the underlined points to generate ideas.

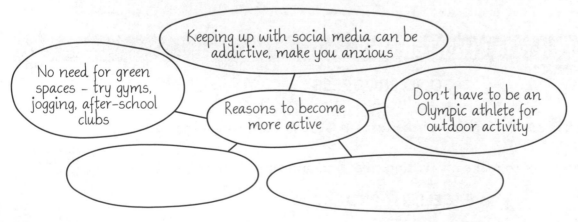

❷ Which two ideas have come from points raised in the question?

❸ Note down two further new points for the article of your own.

You can use the diagram to expand your ideas so that when you come to write about them, you will have even more to say. For example:

However, if the spider diagram takes too long, or doesn't suit your way of working, you can always simply **list your ideas** in note form:

- *Social media = anxious and addictive*
- *No need for green spaces, try clubs, jogging, gyms*
- *Doesn't matter what level you are*

You could also use your spider diagram to simultaneously generate ideas *and* start planning your essay (see more on planning in the next unit). For example, here is a diagram based on the stress of taking a holiday!

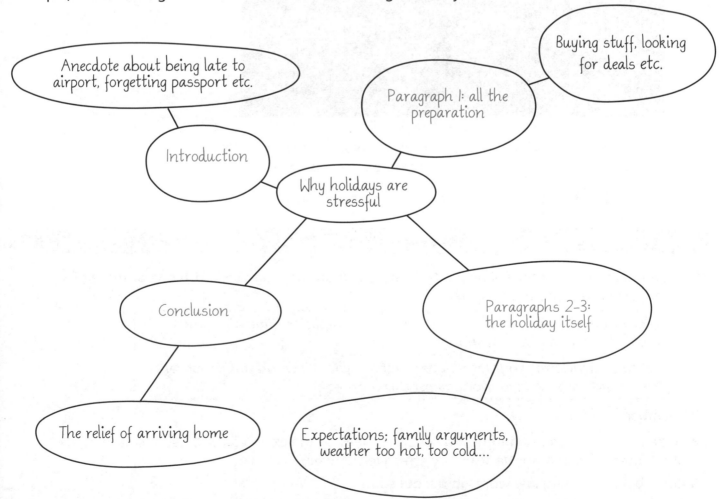

WORD ASSOCIATION

For some types of planning, it helps simply to jot down key words or phrases that come to mind. For example, if you were asked to write a creative piece about a 'holiday that goes badly wrong', you could quickly note down any word associations that come to mind, like this:

break	trip	day out	package holiday	
mum and dad	beach	hotel, half-built	mountain	
ski-ing	instructor	coach	train	airport
flight	passport	tickets		

❹ Write a 50-word outline for a **plot** using two or more of the individual word associations above.

An alternative form of word association is useful in other contexts. For example, if you are given a photo to write about you could take one aspect of it and create more closely linked words (synonyms, for example). There is more on this on page 57, but as an example, consider the image below.

Start with the word 'spray' and find closely linked words (they don't have to be nouns): 'frothy', 'mist', 'shower', 'splattered', 'spreading' etc.

❺ Find linked words for the following nouns: 'stone', 'storm'.

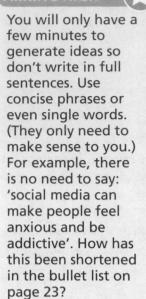

AIMING HIGH ⭐

You will only have a few minutes to generate ideas so don't write in full sentences. Use concise phrases or even single words. (They only need to make sense to you.) For example, there is no need to say: 'social media can make people feel anxious and be addictive'. How has this been shortened in the bullet list on page 23?

APPLYING YOUR SKILLS

❻ Generate ideas for the following GCSE-style English Language task. Use one or more of the techniques you have learned.

> *A proposal has been made to close the local ten-pin bowling alley and replace it with a discount shop.*
>
> *Write an article for your local paper to share your views on this proposal. You could write in favour or against this proposal.*

Remember:

- Take no more than 2–3 minutes to generate ideas (in the exam you will need to save 2 minutes for planning the structure effectively as well).
- Start by underlining key words in the question.

2.2 EFFECTIVE PLANNING

Careful planning helps shape the ideas you have generated effectively. This means deciding on:

- The overall structure of your writing piece – its shape
- The order, sequence or priority of your key ideas or events

KEEPING IT SIMPLE

For the most basic plan, simply number the points or ideas you have generated. This could represent the number of paragraphs (unless you plan to cover more than one point per paragraph) and/or a particular order (for example, by priority). For example, taking the task from page 22, here is one student's plan:

- Social media = anxiety and addictive   1
- No need for green spaces, try clubs, jogging, gyms   4
- Doesn't matter what level you are   3
- Lack of even basic exercise bad for body and emotional well-being.   2
- Discover a passion for something surprising   5

In this example, the structure the student has decided on starts with the problems and moves to the benefits.

❶ Look again at the ideas you generated for Task 6 in 2.1. Create a basic plan by writing numbers next to the points you have made. You could either:

  a) follow the same structure as above (start with the problems, move on to the benefits)

  or

  b) decide what your most important points are and where they should go (beginning, middle or end?)

Alternatively, if you are someone who thinks very visually, draw a simple flow diagram, like the one below, to help you plan.

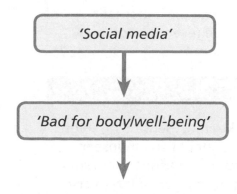

TOP TIP

In some GCSE English Literature essays you may have to write about an extract and then relate your ideas to the rest of the text. In those cases, a clear and logical approach would be to start with points based on the extract before moving on to the whole text.

DIFFERENT FORMS OF WRITING

Your plan and structure will also be determined by the *type* of writing task you are doing. These can sometimes have particular structural conventions or features.

For example, stories are often told in **chronological order**. This can be shown in a useful five-stage plan or **narrative arc**.

1 **Exposition** (characters, setting and situation introduced)
2 **Rising action** (tension builds – conflict or main **complication** arises)
3 **Climax** (defining moment of highest excitement or drama)
4 **Falling action** (tension falls, though some uncertainty remains)
5 **Resolution** (problems resolved – for better or worse)

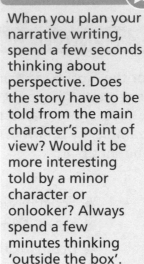

AIMING HIGH

When you plan your narrative writing, spend a few seconds thinking about perspective. Does the story have to be told from the main character's point of view? Would it be more interesting told by a minor character or onlooker? Always spend a few minutes thinking 'outside the box'.

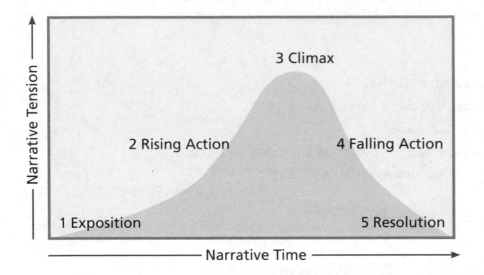

❷ Here is one student's plan for their story, but it is rather mixed up. Where should each of these go on the narrative arc?

> a) Dan meets Jools but they argue when he realises she is daughter of his father's business rival
>
> b) Jools runs away from home
>
> c) Jools's father reconciles with Dan's father. Dan is hopeful Jools will see him one day.
>
> d) Jools agrees to go home but doesn't want to see Dan
>
> e) Jools in danger on the streets – Dan's dad helps him save her.

❸ What would be the benefit of *beginning* with the most dramatic moment in the story about Jools and Dan above (even though in chronological time it takes place later in the story)?

LOGICAL ORDER AND FLEXIBILITY

The logical order for an essay is the one that makes most sense. This might be chronological, but it does not have to be. For example, in an unseen poetry response you might work through the poem, from start to finish, but you could also move from one key idea to another, from a later verse back to an earlier one.

EXAM FOCUS

In the following example, a student has used structure flexibly:

> Suggests analysis will go through poem line by line

The opening line of 'Ozymandias' starts with the narrator's voice stating how he 'met a traveller.' This frames the story that is then told by the speaker who recalls the ruined statue of a long dead king.

By the final line of the poem, the original narrator's voice is completely forgotten - it is the traveller's vision that depicts the 'lone and level sands'. The new voice has transported us away from the original one.

> Jumps from start to end of poem

4 Has the student structured this according to key ideas he/she wants to make, or by tackling every line one by one? What parts of the poem might he/she cover next?

5 Think of at least two ways you could structure a response to a poem you are studying.

APPLYING YOUR SKILLS (A05)

Read the following task:

> 'Cycling should now be banned on all roads, and cyclists should stick to cycle lanes or pavements'.
>
> Write an article for a broadsheet newspaper arguing for or against this point of view.

6 Generate ideas for the article, using one of the techniques from 2.1. Then, decide on the order of the ideas/points and your reason for tackling them in this way.

PROGRESS CHECK FOR CHAPTER TWO

GOOD PROGRESS

I can:

- Generate ideas using a listing or diagrammatic approach ☐
- Organise my ideas into paragraphs ☐

EXCELLENT PROGRESS

I can:

- Consider a range of ways of generating ideas and decide on the best one for me ☐
- Organise my ideas in a range of ways, appropriate to the set task ☐

3.1 WRITING EFFECTIVE SHORT AND LONGER ANSWERS

The different forms, styles and lengths of writing you will produce for GCSE require different skills. It is vital to work efficiently in the time allotted.

SHORT ANSWERS

Some questions in your GCSE English Language exam are worth a small number of marks. This means you must write only what you need to write.

For example, read the following extract from a fictional account of one child's life, and then look at the question that follows it.

> At breakfast a visitor foolish enough to enter the house and go to the kitchen would have been witness to the pile of tottering unwashed pots, the grimy pans and cutlery flung across the table, and the corners of crusts of bread chewed and discarded on the floor. If he had been stupid enough to remain at the doorway, he would have further witnessed the madness of school bus time with a tribe of seven children catapulting their dishes into the sink and knocking over chairs as they trampled over him into the narrow hallway.
>
> As eighth child – and not of school age, Joseph was in effect an invisible child who was perpetually hungry, something he remembered later in life when looking back at his childhood. How awful it had been!
>
> In many ways, Joseph's family has been lucky; there was food, albeit meagre, and they did make it to school, though often without the correct uniform or with ill-fitting shoes or ones with holes in. The toilet was a 'privvy' in the back yard, and the only heating was the coal fire in the parlour. Life was tough.
>
> **1** *List four ways in which the kitchen is in a confused state in the morning.*

EFFECTIVE, SHORT RESPONSES

One of the responses might be:

> It is full of dirty cooking vessels.

Here, there is no need to mention the word 'kitchen' and you can sum up the items as 'dirty cooking vessels' – in other words by using **paraphrase**.

Or you could use **direct quotation**:

> It is full of 'unwashed pots', 'grimy pans' and 'crusts of bread'.

There is no need to mention the visitor passing the door as it is not relevant to the question.

❶   Write a short response answer to each of the following tasks. Either use direct quotation or paraphrase your answers:

   a) *Note down one way a visitor would have been in danger if they had stood in or near the kitchen.*

   b) *In what two ways could Joseph's family be considered lucky?*

LONGER RESPONSES TO TEXTS

Longer responses to reading will range from writing about extracts or short, but complete texts in GCSE English Language to writing about extracts, whole plays, novels and poems in GCSE English Literature. For example, a GCSE English Language task might read:

> *How does the writer use language here to describe Joseph's home life? In your answer you could include the writer's choice of:*
> - *words and phrases*
> - *language features and techniques*
> - *sentence forms.*

For these sorts of question it is important that you:

- Include a **range of ideas** – here, the three bullets suggest what you should cover
- Develop your points **fully** – this means you should not only identify language features, but also comment on their effects
- Draw **overall conclusions,** where appropriate, taking into account the different points you have made

Read the opening paragraph of this response to the question above. Then answer the question that follows it.

> The writer paints a convincing picture of a poor household which is both chaotic and without basic amenities. Adjectives such as 'grimy' and 'unwashed' convey the unclean state of the kitchen, while the reference to 'meagre' food adds to the sense of deprivation. The overall picture is of a tough, uncompromising life in which Joseph seems to suffer more than most.

❷ Evaluate the effectiveness of this response:
- Does it tackle any of the three bullets in the question? If so, which?
- Are there any other points that could have been made?
- Does it simply identify uses of language – or does it analyse?
- Does it draw any overall conclusion about Joseph's life?

APPLYING YOUR SKILLS (A05) (A06)

❸ Now complete the response adding further points related to the language features and sentence forms. Make sure you write a paragraph on each of these.

Remember:
- Include succinct, direct quotation as evidence.
- Alternatively, paraphrase concisely and efficiently.

3.2 WRITING ABOUT FICTION TEXTS

When it comes to fiction – either extracts from novels, or whole novels, there are some important skills you can utilise to clarify your ideas and make clear links across the text.

WHAT YOU HAVE TO WRITE ABOUT

You will be asked questions about how a character, setting or idea is *presented* by the author – either within an extract (for GCSE English Language) or within an extract and/or across a full text (for GCSE English Literature). For example, you may be asked about:

- Your 'impressions': this means 'my understanding of what someone or something is like, based on what the writer tells the reader'
- How events, characters or relationships 'develop': this means 'my understanding of how things change over the course of the text'

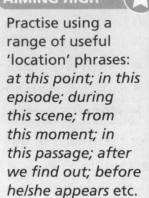

AIMING HIGH

Practise using a range of useful 'location' phrases: *at this point; in this episode; during this scene; from this moment; in this passage; after we find out; before he/she appears* etc.

MAKING PRECISE REFERENCES

In your GCSE English Literature exam, you will have to consider ideas of **characterisation** in relation to an extract and/or across the whole novel. In both cases, this means referring precisely to the context or location for any events or character speech. For example, you might write:

Reference to position in novel

In this episode, which occurs in the graveyard, right at the start of the novel, Magwitch is presented as a terrifying brute ...

Reference to setting or location

Connective signals new point

Later, as Magwitch lies dying in jail in Chapter 56 ...

❶ Choose a character in a novel you are studying who appears more than once. Copy and complete this paragraph about them. (Don't worry about adding any details about their characterisation for now).

.... *is introduced to the reader in* ....

when he/she ....

Later, he/she reappears in ....

when ....

DEVELOPING AN APPROPRIATE VOCABULARY

Whether the text is one you meet as part of English Language or English Literature GCSE, using a rich vocabulary can make your writing sound professional and impressive. For example:

| Alternative word for a 'scene' or a particular passage |

In this episode, Pip is stunned by the appearance of a criminal in chains. Although Magwitch appears at first to be the novel's antagonist, a character who will provide obstacles to Pip's happiness, in reality he proves to be quite different, and Dickens evokes our sympathy for him through his portrayal.

| More formal or academic term for 'villain' |

| Useful term meaning 'brings out' |

| Another word for 'characterisation' |

❷ Can you help this student improve the vocabulary in their opening paragraph? (You don't need to know the novel, *Animal Farm*, to do so!) Copy and complete the paragraph replacing the underlined words with alternatives from the word bank below.

> As the novel <u>starts</u>, Orwell <u>gives</u> a picture of a farm that is poorly run, and <u>presents</u> an owner, Mr Jones who is lazy and ill-tempered. As the <u>first</u> events <u>happen</u>, we see the emergence of characters who will have significant impact on the <u>plot</u>.

describes	culminates	unfold	creates	narrative
conveys	initial	action	opens	events	portrays

TOP TIP ⭐

It can be very easy to mix up terms relating to specific **genres**. So, for example, take care not to refer to 'acts' in novels, or 'chapters' when you are talking about poems or plays.

APPLYING YOUR SKILLS (A01) (A04)

❸ Open a novel or short story you are studying at random. Read from the top of the page for about 100 words. Briefly make a note of what is happening, or is about to happen, and who appears or is speaking. If it is a description, jot down what is being described and why.

Then, write a paragraph in which you succinctly describe what is going on, and what the reader discovers. You could use the paragraph above as a basic structure (with improved vocabulary).

Remember:

● Use 'location' words to show your reader what you are referring to and where/when.

● Comment on what the reader learns from this 100 words about characters, relationships or settings.

3.3 WRITING ABOUT NON-FICTION TEXTS

As with all critical writing when responding to **prose** non-fiction texts, you will need to be clear in what you say and your style should be analytical.

RESPONDING TO OPINION PIECES OR PERSONAL WRITING

In the exam, you will be awarded marks for selecting key information, writing about the particular effects a writer achieves through language choices, comparing viewpoints, and evaluating the effectiveness of an argument.

The key to this is being able to explain explicit (more obvious) information and draw an **inference** from what is implied. How can you do this?

Type of information/ text	Verbs you could use	Example
Commenting on **explicit**/factual information, when the writer's meaning is clear.	The writer … *states, says (not ideal as it could be confused with 'speak out loud'), tells the reader, describes, depicts, shows that, indicates*	*The writer states that the seafront was 'disgusting' and 'overcrowded.'*
Commenting on **implicit** ideas or what a writer feels.	The writer … *suggests, conveys the idea that, implies, gives the impression that, hints, explores*	*The writer suggests the holiday resort is unwelcoming and uncomfortable.*

For example, here is a short extract from a letter from W. D. Howells in 1875 to the writer Mark Twain (whose real name was S. L. Clemens).

My dear Clemens,

The type-writer came Wednesday night, and is already beginning to have its effect on me. Of course it doesn't work: if I can persuade some of the letters to get up against the ribbon they won't get down again without digital assistance[1]. The treadle[2] refuses to have any part or parcel in the performance; and I don't know how to get the roller to turn with the paper. Nevertheless, I have begun several letters to My d ar leman, as it prefers to spell your respected name, and I don't despair yet of sending you something in its beautiful handwriting – after I've had a man out from the agent's to put it in order. It's fascinating, in the meantime, and wastes my time like an old friend.

Glossary:
[1] *digital assistance* – use of fingers
[2] *treadle* – a foot-pedal to operate the 'return' key.

Here are two student responses to a question about *how* the writer conveys his feelings about the typewriter:

Student A

> The writer says that the typewriter is affecting him and that it doesn't work properly. The letters stick on the ribbon and he says the roller won't 'turn with the paper'. He says that it 'wastes' his time.

Student B

> The writer tells the reader that the typewriter is affecting him as it doesn't work properly. He implies that the typewriter has a life of its own as he has to 'persuade' it, and the treadle 'refuses' to do what he wants. However, he says he finds it 'fascinating' and it suggests that he is enjoying getting to grips with it, as he says it is 'like an old friend.'

❶ Which of these two examples states *just* the factual information (i.e. anything that is obvious about the typewriter and how it operates)?

❷ Which focuses mostly on the implicit information (i.e. things that can be inferred from the extract)?

❸ What is different about each student's use of verbs in each case?

❹ Which example better explains the writer's feelings?

TOP TIP

Ensure you check the question carefully. If you are asked to state clear facts (e.g. 'what is wrong with the typewriter') then you don't need verbs which explain things more deeply.

WRITING ABOUT YOUR IMPRESSIONS

Where you are asked directly about your personal opinions, for example, 'What do you think of the writer's views about technology expressed in the letter?', then you can use the **first person** ('I') in your response and verbs such as 'feel', 'think that', 'believe' etc. For example:

> *I feel that the writer's response to the typewriter is understandable, given how these machines would have been very novel and surprising.*

However, if you are asked about the effectiveness of the text – for example, how well the writer conveys his frustrations with the machine, a more analytical and evaluative response is needed. In this case, you might choose to leave out the first person ('I'). For example:

> *I feel that The writer's response to the 'performance' of the typewriter gives a vivid picture of ...*

APPLYING YOUR SKILLS   A06

❺ Below is a student's response to a different article about modern technology. Replace the underlined words with a wider range of verbs in both the implicit and explicit comments that the student has made.

> The writer <u>says</u> that smartphones 'distract' him from 'living' and he <u>says</u> they are like 'a constant child that needs attention.' This <u>says</u> that he feels responsibility but also <u>says</u> that they are a source of irritation.

Remember:

● Some verbs are useful for interpreting language such as 'suggests' or 'implies'.

● When explaining the meaning or quoting, use words such as 'states' or' indicates'.

3.4 WRITING ABOUT POETRY AND DRAMA

Poetry and drama have very specific conventions which require you to approach them in slightly different ways.

GETTING YOUR SUBJECT VOCABULARY RIGHT

It is important that you use an appropriate terminology when you write about the poems and plays you have studied.

Play terms	Poetry terms
act, scene, line, **dialogue, aside, soliloquy, fourth wall**	**stanza**, line, **rhyming couplet, refrain, quatrain, octave, sestet**
character, cast, role,	**rhyme scheme**, rhythm, **metre**, stress, **cadence**,
action, exit, entrance	syllable
staging, prop, costume, design, **stage direction**	**repetition, alliteration, onomatopoeia, caesura, enjambment,**
gesture, **voice**, movement,	**tone**, voice, perspective
Types: tragedy, comedy, romance, **naturalistic,** realist etc.	**Types: lyric, elegy, epic, ballad,** blank verse, **sonnet, free verse** etc.

❶ Do you know what each of these terms means? Check their usage by trying to put each one into a sentence that shows its meaning. For example, 'In the first Act of the play, we are introduced to the main character.'

❷ Are there any other terms you could add to the lists?

TOP TIP

Use the Glossary on page 85 to check the definitions of any highlighted terms you are unfamiliar with.

WRITING ABOUT PLAYS

In plays, as in novels, you may have to trace the development of a particular **character** or **relationship.** However, because the plays you read relate to performance – a living, physical event – it can be very useful to focus on the impact of a character's first appearance (and their exit, if they have one). For example:

> *The fact that the Inspector breaks into what is a private, family celebration when he first appears at the end of Act 1 Scene 1 establishes him immediately as an outsider, someone beyond the control of the Birling empire.*

If you are **tracing a theme or idea,** a key skill is to be able to range across many different moments or conversations in the play. For example:

> *Conflict is apparent from the very first scene of the play when 'rebellious subjects', the Capulets and Montagues, brawl in the streets. It is fitting that in Act 5, Scene 3, the final scene of the play sees the two fathers together again, this time in the 'glooming peace' of the lovers' funeral.*

❸ Copy and complete this table about a major character, and a minor one, from a play you have studied.

Character	When and in what circumstances do they first/last appear?	What does this tell us?
Major		
Minor		

POETRY: BRINGING ALL THE ELEMENTS TOGETHER

When you write about poems from an anthology or unseen ones, character and theme may be relevant, but because poetry texts are more compact and focused, the key is to consider how *all* the different components of the poem come together to explore an idea, or tell a story.

You will need to consider:

- **Content**: every poem has tells a story or has a subject. Even if it is 'a description of how the Autumn makes the poet feel' – that is its 'story'.
- **Language**: what particular vocabulary choices have been made?
- **Literary devices**: what specific techniques has the poet employed (e.g. **imagery**, symbolism, analogy)?
- **Sound**: what is distinctive about the sound – the rhythm, rhyme, **pace**, etc?
- **Structure**: what is notable about the organisation of the words and lines on the page (e.g. patterns, divisions, sequences, repetitions, stanzas, etc.)?

TOP TIP

When you write about plays, make sure you pay due attention to the **stage craft** and any references to gesture or movement. Put your novel essays alongside your play ones: you should be able to tell the difference from the terms used.

EXAM FOCUS

In the following response, a student writes about the opening to the famous poem 'Ozymandias'. Note how he/she has managed to address a wide range of elements in one paragraph.

Deals with the structure – how the poem begins

Focuses on vocabulary choice

> The opening line, 'I met a traveller from an ancient land' immediately engages the imagination – an exotic experience is about to be told by an unnamed person. The adjective 'ancient' also suggests myth and legend. However, the perspective then switches from the poet to the mysterious traveller ...

Analyses the effect

Sums up story of the poem

❹ What new aspect does the final sentence of the paragraph address?

APPLYING YOUR SKILLS

(A01)

❺ Choose one of the poems you have studied, and write a paragraph which explores the opening 4–5 lines. Try to tackle at least two different aspects from the bullet list above.

3.5 SELECTING AND SYNTHESISING INFORMATION

Selecting and **synthesising** information from different sources or sections of one text is a key skill in both GCSE English Language and Literature.

WHAT IS SYNTHESIS?

Synthesis is what happens when you take information from one text or part of a text, put it together with information from another and then draw conclusions.

In **GCSE English Language**, you are likely to have to draw out several points from one or more texts, perhaps comparing or contrasting them. For example, in this type of task:

How do the two writers respond differently to the experience of a parachute jump?

In **GCSE English Literature** you are likely to be synthesising information from within one longer text, for example, 3.2 and 3.4. In poetry, you may have to synthesise information from two poems with similar themes.

CONCISE SYNTHESIS

One of the keys to successful synthesis is to cover points quickly and efficiently, writing no more than is absolutely needed. This is especially true in your GCSE English Language exams.

Text A is an extract from a travel book, *Domestic Manners of the Americans* written by an English woman, Frances Trollope, in 1832. In this part, she describes a meeting of a religious revival group of the time:

A

> *'But how am I to describe the sounds that proceeded from this strange mass of human beings? I know no words which can convey an idea of it. Hysterical sobbing, convulsive groans, shrieks and screams the most appalling, burst forth on all sides. I felt sick with horror. As if their hoarse and overstrained voices failed to make noise enough, they soon began to clap their hands violently ...'*

Text B describes a woman called Lucy's first attendance at a football match:

B

> *'I looked around me. I had expected noise, anger, abusive language. But what I hadn't counted on was anxiety. On either side of me, there was a murmuring wave of discontent: fans bit their fingernails, then gasped with widened eyes, or hid their faces as their team faced an onslaught from their opponents. The fans seemed terrified. Terrified the other team would score ... and the home team would (big drum roll ...) ... lose. I didn't get it.'*

❶ Begin by listing 4 or 5 points made by each writer about the crowd's behaviour:
  ● Text A: *strange mass of people, ...*
  ● Text B: *'anxiety' of crowd, ...*

EXAM FOCUS

Now look at how a student begins a synthesis response comparing the **narrators** in each passage.

> Opening sentence using 'Both' concisely synthesises similarities.

> Connective enables contrast to be made linking first and second narrator

Both narrators are surprised by the behaviour of the crowd, but for different reasons. Trollope is sickened by the sight, whereas Lucy is shocked because the crowd does not behave as she had predicted.

> Adjective sums up Trollope's feelings

> Adjective sums up Lucy's feelings

❷ Write a paragraph comparing the *behaviour* of the two crowds. You can go back to your list of points in task 1.

- Start with a sentence summing up any similarities: *Both crowds seem …*
- Write a second sentence contrasting their behaviour using a connective such as 'however', 'while', 'but' or 'yet.'

SYNTHESISING INFORMATION IN LITERARY TEXTS

When making observations about characters or events across parts of a play or novel, use **noun phrases** to synthesise or sum up ideas. For example:

> *Macbeth's violent treachery in the play so far contrasts strongly with the noble loyalty of Banquo …*

As seen in 1.5, you can also **shorten quotations** to fit the task. For example, if responding to an essay question about Juliet in *Romeo and Juliet*:

Full quotation	Part quotation embedded in a point being made
'Although I joy in thee, I have no joy of this contract tonight, It is too rash, too unadvised, too sudden, Too like the lightning, which doth cease to be Ere one can say 'it lightens.'	Juliet is concerned about how quickly things seem to be progressing between her and Romeo, considering them, 'too rash, too unadvised, too sudden'.

TOP TIP

You can only synthesise information from a text when you are confident about its content so read each source or extract twice before you attempt to synthesise key points.

APPLYING YOUR SKILLS

(A01) (A04)

❸ Take two different characters from a literature text you have studied and write a concluding paragraph in which you discuss their response to the same event.

Remember:

- Try to be efficient in summing up how they react.
- Contrast and draw ideas together using connectives such as 'Both' or 'In each case'.
- If you include a quotation, make it succinct and relevant.

3.6 COMPARING AND CONTRASTING

This skills of comparing and contrasting are relevant to many aspects of GCSE English Language and English Literature.

Sometimes, you may have to compare and contrast **two whole texts** – such as two poems dealing with a similar theme; on other occasions it might be comparing **two extracts**, such as newspaper articles on similar topics.

The other form of comparison is more subtle. It occurs when you are asked to comment on a **particular character** in a text, perhaps focusing on their changing behaviour and the way they are presented **at different times in the story or play**.

In both cases, there are writing techniques you can apply to your sentences, paragraphs or your essay as a whole.

SENTENCE STRUCTURE

Within **sentences**, you can use the order of **clauses**, **conjunctions** and punctuation to address two sides of the argument:

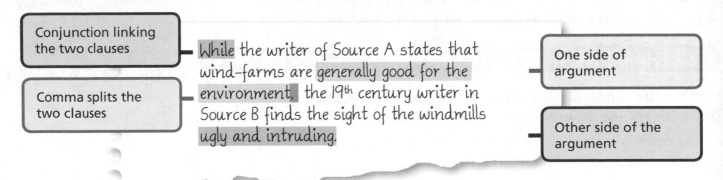

Conjunction linking the two clauses

Comma splits the two clauses

While the writer of Source A states that wind-farms are generally good for the environment, the 19th century writer in Source B finds the sight of the windmills ugly and intruding.

One side of argument

Other side of the argument

This structure also works for literature essays, for example to explain how a character develops:

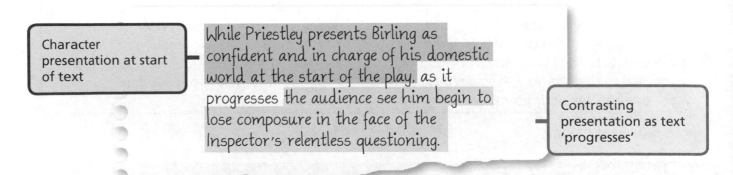

Character presentation at start of text

While Priestley presents Birling as confident and in charge of his domestic world at the start of the play, as it progresses the audience see him begin to lose composure in the face of the Inspector's relentless questioning.

Contrasting presentation as text 'progresses'

❶ Complete this sentence about any character in a play or novel you have studied, using a similar structure to describe change:

Even though at the start of .... the writer

presents .... as.........................., by the time we get to

.. .

PARAGRAPH STRUCTURE

Within paragraphs, you can use a **topic sentence** and contrasting points in further sentences to develop comparison. For example:

> Topic sentence introduces the general issue

> Connective introduces **counter-argument**

Wind energy is an issue both writers feel passionately about. On the one hand, the writer of Source A considers them eco-friendly. However, the writer of Source B, referring to windmills, considers such 'infernal machines' a blight on the landscape.

> Connective at start of second sentence introduces one side of argument

Again, this approach can be applied to literature texts:

Scrooge's transformation is very gradual over the course of the novel. At first, he is emotionally affected by seeing scenes from his past life for example when he 'wept to see his poor forgotten self'. However, by the end he is making a pledge to change his actions, not just how he feels, claiming he is 'not the man' he once was.

TOP TIP

Topic sentences – which indicate the main focus of a paragraph – do not always come at the start. They can be used for summary statements at the end, or even appear in the middle, provided they deal with the general focus or idea, not the specifics.

❷ In the paragraph about Scrooge above, identify:
- The topic sentence
- The time marker which refers to the early part of the novel
- The connective which introduces Scrooge's changed self

Now, read these two short fragments from two poems about Autumn.

> *Seasons of mists and mellow fruitfulness*
> *Close bosom friend of the maturing sun ...*
>
> (from 'To Autumn' by John Keats)

> *Know'st thou not at the fall of the leaf*
> *How the heart feels a languid grief*
>
> (from 'Autumn Song' by Daniel Gabriel Rossetti)

❸ Write a paragraph which:
- Uses a topic sentence to summarise what both poems are about
- Has a second sentence explaining the tone of the Keats extract
- Has a third sentence contrasting it with the tone of the Rossetti extract

❹ Try swapping the order around – does the topic sentence work if you place it at the end?

WHOLE TEXT STRUCTURE

Imagine you have been asked to compare the perspective of two writers on the subject of 'wind energy'. The first is from a 19th century **prose** account of a windmill; the second is a letter to a newspaper about wind turbines.

There are different ways you could structure your response, each with its pros and cons.

> **Structure A: 'two halves'**
>
> Paragraph 1: Introduction
>
> Paragraphs 2-3: How writer of 19th century text presents ideas
>
> Paragraphs 4-5: How writer of modern letter presents ideas
>
> Paragraph 6*: Conclusion
>
> (*You can of course write more paragraphs than this!)

Pros: this approach is easy to follow.

Cons: if you have been specifically asked to make links or directly compare the texts, it can be more difficult.

> **Structure B: 'alternate paragraphs'**
>
> Paragraph 1: Introduction
>
> Paragraph 2: points about 19th century text
>
> Paragraph 3: points about modern letter
>
> Paragraph 4: further points about 19th century text
>
> Paragraph 5: further points about modern text
>
> Paragraph 6: Conclusion

Pros: you can make links between paragraphs, especially where both authors address similar issues.

Cons: the approach is slightly more complicated and the task might not ask you to make specific links.

Both these structures could also work when writing about an extract from a play or novel and the text as a whole.

❹   Choose a character in a text you studied. Either write a paragraph plan
   ● to compare them with another character
   or
   ● to compare how they are presented at the start of the poem, play or novel, and at the end.

> **TOP TIP** ⭐
>
> Highly confident writers can move between points for/ against in viewpoint essays in *each* paragraph, as shown in the wind farms example on page 39, but never lose sight of the focus of the essay.

USING CONNECTIVES

As you have seen, connectives can be useful for comparison. For example:

Comparing similar points	Contrasting ideas or points
In the same way	*However*
Both	*Yet*
Also	*On the one hand/on the other*
Like or *Likewise*	*But*
On both counts	*While*
Neither ...nor (when commenting on how texts or ideas are similar in what they do/don't cover)	*Whereas*
	Although

⑤ Choose appropriate connectives from the table above to complete these points from a non-fiction viewpoint essays:

   a) *According to the first writer .... homework can be good for quick practice of key skills, it is less useful when unfocused and open.*

   b) *The second writer suggests that .... adults and children find smart phones invaluable in daily life, if for different reasons.*

   c) *The writer of the second text states that cycling has become incredibly popular since the 2012 Olympics, ... there are plenty of car drivers who are not so pleased with the numbers of cyclists on the road.*

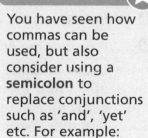

AIMING HIGH

You have seen how commas can be used, but also consider using a **semicolon** to replace conjunctions such as 'and', 'yet' etc. For example:

Most children are increasingly inactive; most parents are increasingly worried.

Genetic crops may solve world food shortages; pressure groups say they are too dangerous.

APPLYING YOUR SKILLS   (A05) (A06)

⑥ Write two paragraphs giving your view on allowing children freedom to play outside on their own.

PROGRESS CHECK FOR CHAPTER THREE

GOOD PROGRESS

I can:

- Apply a range of skills to short and longer responses to fiction, non-fiction, poetry and drama texts ☐
- Synthesise basic points and compare and contrast in a clear and logical way ☐

EXCELLENT PROGRESS

I can:

- Apply a wide range of skills and writing techniques to short and longer responses to fiction, non-fiction, poetry and drama texts ☐
- Synthesise ideas fluently and concisely and draw effective, analytical contrasts and comparisons between texts ☐

4.1 VOCABULARY FOR IMPACT

Your choice of individual words or phrases can have a big impact on what you want to say and alter meaning in subtle or more obvious ways.

WIDE AND SPECIFIC VOCABULARY

Vocabulary usually refers to the selection of specific words or phrases not to sentences or word order. Look at these examples of writing about a party:

> *People were dancing and singing. Then, we all tucked into the food on the table. It was great!*

> *My best friend Paolo was jiggling about like a fish on a line, and my sister Giovanna was bellowing at the top of her voice to her favourite song! Then, we all tucked into the focaccia, sun-dried tomatoes, black olives and creamy pasta shells with ricotta.*

❶ What details are included in the second version but not in the first?

❷ What do these additional details tell us?

In the example above, the details of Italian food, the names and roles of the people ('best friend' and 'sister'), and the verb choices ('jiggling about' and 'bellowing') all tell us *what* or *how*. (What people? What food? How were they dancing/singing?)

❸ Improve this further paragraph from the same account by replacing the underlined words or phrases. Use the word bank below, or choose your own to fit the situation.

> *Suddenly there was a huge <u>noise</u>. With all the dancing, a <u>piece of furniture</u> had <u>fallen</u> over and <u>went</u> onto the floor. My father <u>came</u> into the room. 'What's going on?' he <u>said</u>, angrily.*

whisper	bang	crack	clatter	vase
wardrobe	grandfather clock	shelf	crashed
toppled	flopped	slammed	ambled	ran
burst	strode	raced	cried	murmured
	croaked	demanded		

NOUN PHRASES

Noun phrases are a particularly effective way of building vocabulary. For example, take the noun 'tomatoes'. We can create phrases by adding adjectives or other phrases:

Sun-dried tomatoes (one adjective added)

Juicy sun-dried tomatoes (two adjectives added)

Juicy sun-dried tomatoes shining in the sun

(two adjectives + **participle** verb + prepositional phrase)

❹ Take any noun from the word bank above and create a noun phrase from it in the same way.

SYNONYMS AND SENSES

It is useful to develop a rich vocabulary related to the senses. For example here are just a few of the adjectives associated with taste:

> *hot, spicy, fresh, tangy, acidic, bitter, juicy, luscious*

Some of these are **synonyms**, which are very useful when you want to enrich your writing.

❺ Which of the 'taste' words above are synonyms?

❻ Practise your 'sense skills' by writing two paragraphs about being lost in a rainforest. You could use this photo for some ideas.

TOP TIP

Focus in on categories *within* the senses (for example, colours or shapes for 'sights', or scent of flowers for 'smell' etc.)

- In paragraph 1: describe the *sights* you see. Focus on colour, and use unusual ones (e.g. 'indigo') or ones related to jewels (e.g. 'emerald'). You may need to research rainforest vocabulary for plants.
- In paragraph 2 choose **one** of the other senses (the *sounds* you hear, the *touch* of things around you, the *taste* of things or the *smells* you encounter) and describe your experiences.

You could build noun phrases to make your descriptions come to life.

AIMING HIGH

Try out closely related words when you write practice pieces for GCSE to see how you can subtly alter the effect you are trying to create. For example, in the rainforest text you could use the adjectives 'quiet' or 'stealthy' to describe a jaguar. What would be the difference?

POSITIVE AND NEGATIVE CONNOTATIONS

The words you choose can also have positive and negative **connotations** (or be fairly neutral).

❼ Which of the following adjectives for a person who likes to talk are most positive or negative?

> *loud-mouthed; talkative; chatty; gossipy; verbose, communicative*

❽ Choose any one of these words and write a sentence from the opening to a story which makes the meaning clear.

APPLYING YOUR SKILLS

❾ Write 75–100 words describing someone's experiences of being lost in a desert or wilderness.

Remember:

- Use specific rather than general vocabulary (e.g. 'scorpion' rather than 'insect').
- Refer vividly to the senses to suit the situation.

4.2 SENTENCES FOR VARIETY AND EFFECT

By selecting from a range of styles and lengths of sentence you can create different meanings and make an impact on your reader.

LENGTH OF SENTENCES

At the most basic level, using both short and long sentences can create particular effects. For example:

> Long drawn-out first sentence of linked actions involving great effort

> I struggled through the remaining undergrowth, pulled myself up by the low-hanging branches and clambered up the final wet, slippery section to the top where I flopped over the edge and lay gasping, the sky clear and bright above me. I had done it.

> Final short sentence emphasises the end – the explorer's ordeal is over

Here, the final effort to achieve the last part of the climb is *continuous* – the first 'struggle' links to the 'clamber' and then to the 'flop' over the edge.

However, short sentences could also be used to show a different sort of struggle:

> I surveyed the combination on the safe. I put my ear to the dial, and began to turn it. First, a few notches to the right. I stopped. Listened. Was that a click? I turned the dial again, the opposite way. Another click. Finally, I continued clockwise for a few more notches. Listened closely. Click. Yes! Suddenly, the door swung open. I had done it!

❶ Why are shorter sentences especially effective here? What do they convey to the reader about the writer's situation and actions?

❷ The writer uses a number of **minor sentences** here – i.e. short, grammatically incomplete sentences. Can you identify them?

❸ Now, write a paragraph describing someone trying to reach a puppy that has fallen down the bank near a fast-moving stream. Start with:

I slowly inched forward...

- Use short sentences to begin with to describe the act of reaching the puppy.

- Then use a longer sentence to describe a moment at the end when the puppy almost slips as you try to capture it.

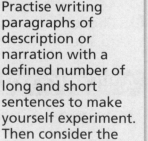

AIMING HIGH

Practise writing paragraphs of description or narration with a defined number of long and short sentences to make yourself experiment. Then consider the effect.

EXAM FOCUS

In viewpoint essays, you can use the three main sentence types (check 1.3) to help organise your ideas or promote your particular opinion. For example, read this extract from one student's essay:

Simple sentence states point clearly

Complex sentence develops argument and provides detailed evidence

The facts are clear. Fast food may be cheap but it is also harmful. Although we seem to accept it as a normal part of life, research has shown just how high the levels of sugar and salt are in such products.

Compound sentence gives us two of these 'facts'

❹ Using the example above as a model, turn the long sentence below into a paragraph of three sentences. (You may need to remove certain words or add some of your own.)

We must look at ourselves because each day we make decisions about where we buy products and we make choices about what we eat and despite warnings from health professionals about diabetes and heart disease we continue to disregard our own bodies.

ACTIVE AND PASSIVE

You could also consider using the **passive voice** or **active voice** for effect in your sentences. For example:

● 'we make decisions' = active voice (includes the 'do-er' of the action – the subject)

● 'decisions are made' = passive voice (does not say who makes the decision)

This can be useful when writing about unknown causes or when you want to emphasise a particular idea. For instance, look at these three headlines:

A JUNK FOOD DESTROYS YOUNG LIVES

B YOUNG LIVES DESTROYED BY JUNK FOODS

C YOUNG LIVES DESTROYED

❺ Which of the headlines, A, B and C, is in the active and passive voice? Where – or what – is the emphasis in each case?

❻ What is the effect of leaving out the 'do-er' altogether in the third example?

APPLYING YOUR SKILLS

(A06)

❼ Write 60–85 words on the pros or cons of internet shopping. Include all three main sentence types, and if appropriate, a minor sentence for effect.

4.3 PUNCTUATION FOR CLARITY AND CREATIVITY

You can use different forms of punctuation to clarify ideas or change the tone or mood of a text.

CREATING MEANING WITH PUNCTUATION

You can refer back to 1.6 to see how to use punctuation correctly, but punctuation exists for several different reasons. For a start, omitting punctuation can make ideas confused:

> *I find internet shopping is completely addictive flicking through screens zooming in on fabrics and comparing prices for hours wastes time.*

Here, the key point needs to be made obvious, and the supporting points separated into manageable 'chunks' of text. For example:

> *I find internet shopping is completely addictive. Flicking through screens, zooming in on fabrics and comparing prices for hours wastes time.*

❶ What punctuation has been added?

❷ Where could a **colon** have been used?

QUESTIONS FOR IMPACT

Sentence style and punctuation choice go hand in hand. For example, look at how in this example using several **rhetorical questions** (and therefore question marks) one after the other can build up an effect.

> *Should we just sit back and accept the dominance of smart-phones? Why not have a weekend free of them? But would it drive us crazy, I wonder?*

❸ How has the final question been used differently?

❹ Complete this paragraph from a story using a similar structure:
> *Should I just accept that she wasn't going to come? Why not ...?*

TOP TIP

Take care that you use questions sparingly for overall impact. One paragraph like this is just about acceptable, but in general it's best to keep to a minimum.

EXAM FOCUS

Look at how punctuation is used for clarity and to help develop ideas in this response:

> In this extract Macbeth's choice is clear: should he go ahead with the murder, or listen to his conscience? It seems as if conscience is winning when he talks of the 'double trust' the King has shown in him, but when Lady Macbeth appears things change. She mocks him ('Art thou afeard?'), questions his love for her ('Such I account thy love') and finally convinces him ('we'll not fail').

Question mark correctly used

Comma comes before new clause signalling change in scene

Colon introduces the choice

Quotation marks around words from text

⑤ What other punctuation marks are used in the final sentence? For what reason?

⑥ Select one of the texts you have studied, and write a paragraph about a moment when the main character changes or realises something. Start with:

At this moment …

TOP TIP ⭐

Don't over-use exclamation marks in exciting or dramatic stories otherwise the effect can be as if the story is being shouted out loud.

PUNCTUATION IN STORIES

Accurate punctuation is your first priority, but bear in mind how you can use it creatively too. Note how it has been done in this example:

Exclamation marks stress the peril of the situation

Ellipses mimic the horse slowing down – also creates sense of expectation

The horse wouldn't stop! It crashed through branches, leapt over ditches, tore through brambles and vaulted over hedges (nearly throwing me off at least twice in the process) before slowly coming to a halt …

I pulled myself up. Why was there nothing in front of us? All I could see was blue – miles and miles of it – stretching into the distance. Then I looked down: we were on the edge of a cliff, a hundred feet above the rocks and crashing sea!

Brackets are used around text which adds further detail

Text in dashes to emphasise the extent of the 'blue'

⑦ What other punctuation marks been used here? To what effect?

APPLYING YOUR SKILLS   (AO6)

⑧ Continue the story about the wild horse above. Write about how you try to coax and persuade the horse to come away from the edge. Think about how you might use:

- Dashes and ellipses to indicate hesitation or a careful way of speaking
- Brackets for any additional information or to stress an idea
- One exclamation mark only for something shocking or dramatic

You could begin:

I began to whisper in the horse's ear …

4.4 PARAGRAPHS FOR ORGANISATION AND SEQUENCE

Paragraphs are needed not simply to organise your thoughts so that a reader can follow them, but also to create effects.

PARAGRAPH PURPOSES

Paragraphs are generally used when you wish to:

- Introduce a **new, related** or **contrasting point** or **idea**
- Introduce a **new character** or **viewpoint**
- Change the **time** (**flashforwards** or **flashback**) or **location** (from inside to outside, between rooms, or from one place to an entirely different one)
- Change the **mood, pace** or **tone** (usually as a result of the above)

❶ Which of the above has this student used in his story opening?

> Dev and I grew up on the same street, went to the same schools and shared the same interests – even, once, the same house when my parents went away. But all that changed when he was expelled. And it was all my fault.
>
> It was the last day of the term before Christmas. The exams were finished (hooray!) and Dev and I were standing in the Hall. That was when I had the stupid idea to steal the school Christmas tree ...

By moving the focus you can direct the reader's attention: take them to one place, then another, then fast-forward in time or pause to describe something new. Using paragraphs in this way is like steering a boat.

PARAGRAPH FOCUS AND ORDER

In stories, being clear about what each paragraph's focus is can really help. For example, here is part of a plan for the story above:

Para	Time	Place	Focus	Tone
1	Now	None, really – just makes it clear it is in the present day.	Introducing friend Dev, and telling reader the narrator and he aren't friends any more.	Sad, reflective
2	Before Xmas (so back in time)	School – the Hall	The decision that led to Dev being expelled. Dev had always wanted a Xmas tree – narrator had decided how to get one!	Fun, lively
3	Later that same day	Outside school – then the corridor, then the Hall	The boys come back in darkness and sneak into school.	Tense, dramatic

❷ Could the story begin at a different point (e.g. in paragraph 2 or 3)? What would the effect be?

❸ What could go in paragraphs 4 and 5? How might the story develop?

PARAGRAPHS IN VIEWPOINT ESSAYS

The focus of each paragraph and the order of the ideas both *in* and *between* paragraphs are also vital in a viewpoint essay. For example, here is one student's plan for a speech about the importance of team sports.

Paragraph	Focus	Example
1	Introducing the argument	*Not everyone likes team sports but they are a huge part of our lives.* **[1]** *Whether it is watching Premier League football on TV, or playing netball for your school team you cannot avoid them. But should you take part?*
2	1st point: team sports foster cooperation and support fellow team members.	
3	2nd point: everyone gets to participate	
4	3rd point: good social side/ make friends	
5		

In the paragraph 1 example, the highlighted **topic sentence [1]** tells us what the focus of the paragraph is. Here, it is introducing the topic of team sports and rather than saying whether they are good or bad, it provides a general introduction.

❹ Write down at least one more point in favour of team sports for the plan.

Counter-arguments (in this case, against) can be included in the same paragraph, if you wish. For example:

TOP TIP ⭐

Using the simple 'one point per paragraph' approach also works well for literature essays but take care that you allow space for alternative interpretations or ideas.

Topic sentence ⟶ The best teams foster cooperation and in difficult circumstances support their fellow players. Yet, some say that the downside of being in a team is when you are left out and don't get to play. However, a good team and manager can make everyone feel involved, and help support the team regardless of who is selected.

Counter-argument

Answer to the counter-argument

APPLYING YOUR SKILLS (A05)

❺ Write the remaining paragraphs from the viewpoint essay (Paragraph 2 onwards). When you have finished, think about whether the order works for you: would you place a different point first, or are you happy with the sequence in the plan?

4.5 CONNECTIVES FOR COHESION

Connectives – linking words or phrases – provide **cohesion** as signposts that allow your reader to follow your train of thought.

CONNECTIVES FOR BUILDING AN ARGUMENT

Connectives have different functions, but one that you are bound to want to use is that of strengthening or developing points. For example, here is one student tracing the main character's ambitions in the play *Macbeth*:

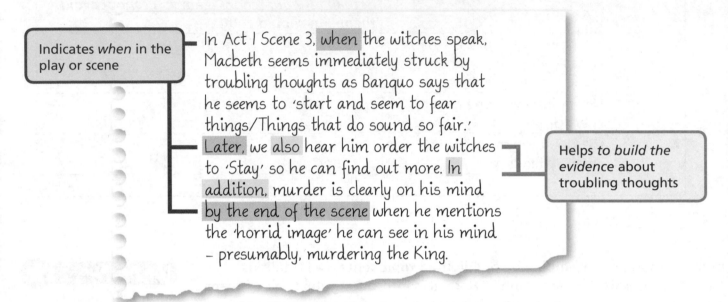

Indicates *when* in the play or scene

In Act I Scene 3, when the witches speak, Macbeth seems immediately struck by troubling thoughts as Banquo says that he seems to 'start and seem to fear things/Things that do sound so fair.' Later, we also hear him order the witches to 'Stay' so he can find out more. In addition, murder is clearly on his mind by the end of the scene when he mentions the 'horrid image' he can see in his mind – presumably, murdering the King.

Helps *to build the evidence* about troubling thoughts

Helping the reader trace the argument in this way is very effective. Other connectives linked to development or tracing an idea like this are:

Time	firstly, secondly, finally, next, then, ultimately, in the end
Building evidence	moreover, furthermore, what is more, and, to add to that, in the same way

❶ Write a paragraph about a character in a text you have studied explaining either their good or bad side. Use at least one 'time' connective and one 'building evidence' connective.

CONNECTIVES FOR COMPARISON AND CONTRAST

Equally important for your critical or viewpoint essays are connectives which help you explain similarities and differences. The most useful ones are:

Similarity	like, in the same way, both, neither, too, also, in both cases
Difference	unlike, however, yet, on the one hand/on the other hand, than, in contrast, but, whereas

❷ Copy and complete this paragraph from a GCSE English Language essay about cycling using appropriate connectives.

.... cycling and driving cars can be dangerous activities. ...., it is clear that if you are on a bike, you have less protection .... car drivers. There is also the issue of visibility. ...., cars have multiple mirrors, ... bikes have none or very few.

CONNECTIVES FOR CAUSE AND EFFECT

Being able to indicate what the outcome of something will be, or explain the motive of a character, requires different connectives to help your text knit **cohesively** together.

For instance: *because, for this reason, as a result, so, consequently, thus, therefore,* are all words or phrases which can help in this way. For example:

> *Because of the investment in sport before the London Olympics in 2012, British athletes did better than ever before.*

> *There was great expectation before the Rio Olympics that British athletes would do well, so perhaps we were not that surprised by the outstanding results.*

> *I'd prepared for years; consequently on the big day I performed well.*

'IF' CLAUSES

A slightly different form of cohesion can be achieved by the useful 'if', or **conditional clause**, which expresses different conditions of cause and effect. For example:

Condition	Construction	Example
Probable to fulfil	Simple present tense	If they *practise*, they *will* win.
In theory, possible	Simple past tense	If they *practised*, they *would* win.
Not possible (too late)	Past perfect tense	If they *had practised*, they *would have won*.

3 Copy and complete this paragraph of 'cause and effect' statements. Use connectives or 'if' clauses or verbs.

I want to talk to you about fitness. .... of Laura Kenny's success, I took up cycling. .... I am now a regular member of my cycling team. .... you take it up, you .... enjoy it just as much as I do.

APPLYING YOUR SKILLS (A05) (A06)

4 Write the closing paragraph of a speech to your schoolmates in which you express your views about the impact of the Olympics on your life (or its lack of impact!). Include:

- At least one connective which contrasts two ideas or points
- One cause and effect connective
- At least one 'if' clause

4.6 SIMILE, METAPHOR AND OTHER LANGUAGE TECHNIQUES

Successful writers use a range of specific techniques which are particularly effective for enlivening or enriching their writing. Often these have the effect of making descriptions more vivid, or persuasive ideas more emotive.

SIMILE AND METAPHOR

Similes are when you use 'like' or 'as' to compare two normally unrelated things: for example;

> *'The town council is like a rudderless ship – it has no idea where it is going, or what it is aiming for.'*

> *'Your face....is as a book where men may read strange matters*,' (Lady Macbeth to Macbeth, suggesting that he needs to hide his feelings).

Metaphors are a strengthened form of simile. They do not say that one thing is like another but that it *is* the other thing. Metaphorical language can also rely on verbs and adjectives, not just nouns.

> *The town council is a rudderless ship, sinking through lack of leadership.*

> *'I have night's cloak to hide me …'* (Romeo to Juliet); the night does not literally wear a cloak but the metaphor creates a vivid image of the darkness wrapped around Romeo.

❶ Complete these similes or metaphors:

The curving river sparkled like ....

Tiny leaping fish were .... *arrows. The sun's rays* ....

A narrow, pointed boat ....*through the water*

like ....

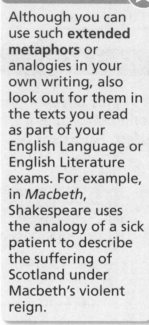

AIMING HIGH

Although you can use such **extended metaphors** or analogies in your own writing, also look out for them in the texts you read as part of your English Language or English Literature exams. For example, in *Macbeth*, Shakespeare uses the analogy of a sick patient to describe the suffering of Scotland under Macbeth's violent reign.

ANALOGY

Analogy is a more extended form of simile and/or metaphor which creates a series of links between two different things. For example:

> *The heart is the capital city of the body, with veins like roads carrying their precious cargo to outlying places. If the capital comes under attack, so the whole kingdom suffers.*

❷ Continue the analogy by completing this sentence:

The pulse throbs like a ....

....

SYMBOLISM

Symbols are descriptions of objects or natural elements that stand for abstract ideas. For example, in Shelley's poem 'Ozymandias', a huge fallen statue in the desert, with words on its base, is described:

> 'My name is Ozymandias, king of kings:
>
> Look on my works, ye Mighty, and despair!'
>
> Nothing beside remains: round the decay
>
> Of that colossal wreck, boundless and bare,
>
> The lone and level sands stretch far away.

The fallen statue could be said to symbolise:

- the way all great empires eventually fail
- or perhaps the arrogance of mankind. Or both!

❸ Here, a writer has used a number of items to symbolise absence. Copy and complete the description:

She opened the bedroom door. On the floor, an abandoned ....

lay on its side. On the unmade bed, the pillow still showed the imprint

of .... The window was half-open and outside on the

tree she could see ....

TOP TIP

Symbolism is often a matter of interpretation, so when you use it in your own writing be aware that you might convey a range of different ideas.

PERSONIFICATION

Personification is a particular form of metaphor which describes non-human or inanimate things as if they were people, or had human characteristics. For example:

> The walls of the city, like huge muscular arms, kept the citizens in their vice-like grip.

In Wordsworth's poem 'Daffodils' he says of the flowers:

> Ten thousand saw I at a glance,
>
> Tossing their heads in sprightly dance.

Note how this student has used personification in this viewpoint essay:

> It is as if litter has invaded our town, set up camp in our streets and smothered and choked our parks. Litter has a vast army, and we seem unable to fight back.

❹ How has litter been personified here?

❺ Can you continue the personification by adding a sentence suggesting the way litter moves or changes when the wind blows?

SOUND EFFECTS: ALLITERATION, ASSONANCE AND ONOMATOPOEIA

It is easy to focus on visual description, but don't forget that writers use sound creatively, too.

Alliteration is when a series of words beginning with the same letter or sound is used for effect. For example:

> *The knight stabbed, slashed and sliced his way through the wall of thorns in front of him.* (The use of the 's' sound here also mimics the sharp thrusts of the sword.)

Often alliteration makes the phrase or line memorable. For example, the **narrator** reminds us that Jacob Marley (in *A Christmas Carol*) was 'dead as a doornail'.

Assonance is the use of similar sounds made by syllables in nearby words. For example:

> *The deep, green sea rose to welcome me.*

But it also can be the use of identical consonant sounds in different words. For example:

> *The story of that starry night starkly shines in my memory.*

Onomatopoeia is when the words used sound like the thing or the action they describe. For example, in this famous poem called 'The Highwayman' by Alfred Noyes:

> *Over the cobbles he clattered and clashed in the dark inn-yard,*
>
> *He tapped with his whip on the shutters, but all was locked and barred;*
>
> *Tlot tlot, tlot tlot! Had they heard it? The horse-hooves, ringing clear;*
>
> *Tlot tlot, tlot tlot, in the distance! Were they deaf that they did not hear?*

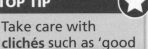

TOP TIP

Take care with **clichés** such as 'good as gold' or 'busy as a bee.' Although alliterative, they may have lost their effect through overuse.

6 Copy and complete this paragraph choosing onomatopoeic words from the word bank below.

The kettle .... as the steam burst out, and old Ma Smith tottered across the floor slowly, ... for breath as she did so. By the time she got to the old stove, the water had boiled dry and when she lifted the spout, only a tiny .... came out. Outside in the yard, a hen .... in its repetitive way, and the little stream by the gate .... happily.

hissed	boiled	pausing	gasping	amount	dribble
	clucked	complained	gurgled	flowed	

RHETORICAL QUESTIONS AND PATTERNS OF THREE

Sound effects are not just for creative/imaginative writing: you can use them in viewpoint writing, too. For example:

I believe the decision is muddled, misguided and morally wrong.

As you can see a pattern of three adjectives that all begin with the same sound adds even more impact here.

Another device is the **rhetorical question**. This is a question in which the answer is expected or 'understood'. You will have already seen it used in 4.3. For example:

Is it right that we should allow this ancient woodland that has nourished so many species, to die?

(Clearly the speaker is expecting his or her **audience** to agree that it is not.)

Or, in a story:

'How can you be so cruel as to lock me in here?' she demanded, as her jailer slammed the door.

Patterns of three (as in the 'muddled, misguided and morally wrong' example above) provide a series of sequential points or ideas, like knocking on a door three times. For example:

The ancient woodland nourishes life, [1] provides a place of reflection, [2] and is beautiful to observe. [3]

APPLYING YOUR SKILLS (A05) (A06)

7 Now write 75–100 words using some of the language devices you have learned about. Either:

- *Write the opening to a descriptive piece about a local wood or forest in the winter.*

or:

- *Write part of a speech to the council arguing that it is/isn't acceptable to build new homes for young people in the countryside around your village/town.*

Remember:

- Use at least two language devices, one of which must be a sound effect.
- Make sure you choose your words or phrases carefully (avoid clichés and use rhetorical devices sparingly so as not to overwhelm the reader).

4.7 WRITING A DESCRIPTIVE TEXT

It is important that you can draw together the skills you have learned for describing a setting, person or situation in a vivid and interesting way. This might be as part of a narrative text (a story) or as a whole text in which the focus is on describing rather than recounting a series of events.

WHAT MAKES AN EFFECTIVE DESCRIPTION?

The most effective descriptive texts:

- Create a **memorable idea or picture** in the reader's mind
- **Focus on details** – although the larger picture is also important
- Allow the reader to **visualise** the thing or person described
- Often draw on the other **senses** – **sound, touch, smell** and/or **taste** to create an impact
- Use carefully chosen **language techniques**, such as **imagery**, alliteration, varied sentences lengths, etc.

Consider this photo, and the two descriptions that follow it.

Student A

> The black branches of the trees shake their icy locks over the curved bridge. Like skeletal spiders, they watch over the frozen waters. The pale sun gazes down. The earth sleeps. The snow sleeps. The winter air hisses.

Student B

> In the park, everything was white and it was cold. Suddenly a person ran across the bridge and raced through the trees, scaring everyone away. Then she went out of the gate and into the city.

❶ Which of these two descriptions is the more effective, based on the bullet list at the top of the page?

❷ What are the weaknesses of the other description?

❸ What effective descriptive features can you identify in the stronger description?

USING THE SENSES

Sight, sound, touch, taste and smell can all be explored as part of a vivid description, but you must make sure they are appropriate. For example, look at these two **similes**:

Simile	Effect
The snow is crisp and clean, like the icing on a wedding cake ...	**Good**
The snow is crisp and clean, like a wobbly creamy balloon ...	**Not so good** (balloons aren't 'crisp' to the touch)

❹ What senses are evoked by this photo? Write annotations for the photo with your own ideas for each of the senses. Bear in mind you will have to imagine things such as sound, touch etc.

Sight:

Smell:

Sound: *roar and hiss of the flame*

Taste:

Touch or texture:

POWERFUL LANGUAGE TECHNIQUES

Descriptive writing is often at its most effective when it creates an impact through an original or interesting depiction of a person or place. The use of powerful language techniques can assist in this. For example, you could use some of the techniques you have learned about in this chapter:

Technique	Example	Effect
simile	[trees] ... *like skeletal spiders*	Conveys the look of their thin bony branches
metaphor	*...shake their icy locks*	Adds to the idea of the trees as living beings with hair – this personifies them
repetition	The earth *sleeps.* The snow *sleeps.*	Stresses the quiet slumber of the scene
onomatopoeia	The winter air *hisses.*	Sound of the verb 'hisses' reflects its meaning, so we hear the wind too

❺ Write an additional paragraph for either the wintry park photo or the one of the fire-eater and include at least one simile/metaphor, one use of repetition and one use of onomatopoeia.

STRUCTURING DESCRIPTION

Description is like holding a camera. Ranging between single words or phrases, sentences or paragraphs, you can point it in different directions, zoom in, zoom out – then pan across to another thing you want to describe.

EXAM FOCUS

Read another sentence from an effective description based on the wintry park:

Takes a general detail from the photo

Offers an imagined detail (cannot be seen in photo)

Under the thick crust of snow, a fragile bluebell tries to force its thin stem up through the surface, reaching for the distant sun.

Zooms in on detail

6 What other 'imagined detail', which *isn't* in the park photo, is described in the sentence?

7 Choose one of these things that are *not* in the photo, and write at least one further sentence about it. Try to focus on one specific aspect of it (for example, the crow's eye).

> a crow   a running shoe   a rusty spade   icicles
> a sign on the bridge   a fox

In longer descriptions, you need to plan what will be covered in each of your paragraphs. For example, imagine you are describing a ship at the dock about to set off on a long voyage.

8 Copy and complete the plan below, adding any further ideas for who or what you would describe. Remember, only start a new paragraph for a reason – to introduce a new focus on a different person, another place or a change in time (e.g. the same scene an hour later).

AIMING HIGH ★

Build precise descriptions around the noun using **adjectives** or **prepositions** in the same way as shown here: 'under **(preposition)** the thick **(adjective)** crust **(noun)** of snow'.

Introduction – Paragraph 1	View of the whole ship from end to end, as seen by someone saying goodbye
Paragraph 2	Shift focus to the person waving goodbye, or someone else on the quayside
Paragraph 3	
Paragraph 4	
Paragraph 5	

EXAM FOCUS

Read this start of a short story called 'The Stranger' by Katherine Mansfield. A student has annotated the extract to highlight the use of structure.

Introduces the overall scene – of a ship being watched by a crowd (wide angle of whole scene)

Creates atmosphere, referring back to the previous paragraph

Offers close-up giving specific details of what the man is like

It seemed to the little crowd on the wharf that she was never going to move again. There she lay, immense, motionless on the grey crinkled water, a loop of smoke above her, an immense flock of gulls screaming and diving after the galley droppings at the stern. You could just see little couples parading—little flies walking up and down the dish on the grey crinkled tablecloth. Other flies clustered and swarmed at the edge. Now there was a gleam of white on the lower deck—the cook's apron or the stewardess perhaps. Now a tiny black spider raced up the ladder on to the bridge.

In the front of the crowd a strong-looking, middle-aged man, dressed very well, very snugly in a grey overcoat, grey silk scarf, thick gloves and dark felt hat, marched up and down, twirling his folded umbrella. He seemed to be the leader of the little crowd on the wharf and at the same time to keep them together. He was something between the sheep-dog and the shepherd.

Switches focus to people on the ship, described like 'flies' (a long-distance shot)

Zooms in on a new person in new paragraph

⑨ Write a paragraph explaining how this description is effectively structured, using some or all of the annotations. You could start:
As the extract opens, the reader seems to be watching the ship and the crowd on the wharf from a distance...

APPLYING YOUR SKILLS

⑩ Write a description of 3 or 4 paragraphs based around the arrival of a luxury car (and its occupant) at a poor, run-down house in a town.

Remember to:

- Plan your paragraphs – what will the focus be in each?
- Zoom in and out, from the 'big' picture to little details.
- Use a wide range of descriptive language techniques and effects.
- Appeal to the senses, where you can.

 TOP TIP

It is important you structure your writing too! Always check your work to see that any new paragraphs begin on a new line, and make sure you have 'indented' the first new line of the paragraph from the margin.

4.8 WRITING A NARRATIVE OR SHORT STORY

Writing a narrative in a short space of time can be challenging but, by focusing carefully on some key ideas, you can create a story that is interesting and effective.

WHAT MAKES AN EFFECTIVE NARRATIVE?

The most effective short stories or narratives:

- Have a **compelling opening** that engages the reader immediately
- Focus on **one** (or at most **two**) **main character(s)** or **protagonists**
- Have a **clear structure** – with some sort of complication, conflict or problem at its heart that needs to be overcome
- Feature **a mix** of **vivid description**, **relevant action** – and, often, **dialogue**
- **End** in a **satisfying**, if **not always happy, way**
- Use carefully selected **language techniques**, such as **imagery**, alliteration, varied sentences lengths, etc.

❶ Which of the following openings from two stories is the more effective? As you read, consider:

- How easily you can picture the situation in your mind
- Which one establishes a clear central character
- Which one grabs your attention
- Which one uses the more vivid description

Student A

> Billy, Dave and Rav were told by their teacher that because of the outbreak of flu they needed volunteers to bat in the cricket match against Norlinton High, the big school nearby. Dave wondered if he'd be 'chosen'. So did Rav. Both were rubbish at sport.

Student B

> The ball whistled past my head like a red bullet. The large boy at the other end of the pitch sniggered unpleasantly. Not for the first time I asked myself how I'd got myself into this position. After all, everyone knew I was the worst at sport in the school.

Both story openings indicate what the problem or complication is, but only one really engages the reader's interest by plunging us straight into the action – or *in media res* as it is sometimes known.

Openings do not have to feature an exciting or dramatic event, but if you are going to begin with a descriptive setting, for example, make sure it is vivid and unusual. Look at 4.5 for help on how to do this.

TOP TIP

Withholding information – not revealing key points straightaway – can also help to engage the reader's attention.

CHARACTER AND VOICE IN STORIES

You can choose to tell your story from any point of view. In fact sometimes choosing a less obvious **narrator** or central character can be very interesting. Look at this image:

Imagine this is the story of a break-up. Read these four extracts all told from different perspectives and in different voices.

> **A** *She sat there, her freckled cheeks paler than usual, and after stirring her coffee and not meeting my eyes, finally told me it was over. I felt a deep, tugging ache low in my stomach, like I'd been punched.*

> **B** *Everyday they came in – the same time, same table. Smiling, holding hands. Happy in their little world. But not today. No, today he saw that something was wrong.*

> **C** *Ella couldn't work out in her mind how he was taking it. He hadn't said anything, just nodded when she explained why they had to split up. Her coffee had gone cold – like their relationship.*

> **D** *I mean I don't like to eavesdrop, and my hearing's not that good any more but you can't help yourself, can you? As I told a man on the bus on the way home, 'Young people are so nasty nowadays...'. He wasn't listening, mind.*

Each of these extracts uses:

● Either the **first person** (I, me, our) or **third person** (He, she, they) narrative

● Different **voices** (ways of speaking/writing as a result of the vocabulary or style of sentences)

❷   Which **narrator** best fits with the people in the picture? In what ways is each narrator's voice different?

Character is made up of other elements as well as voice. For example:

- How a character **behaves** – the things they do, how they move and act
- How a character **looks** – face, body, clothing
- How **others speak** and **respond** to them

How is this achieved in the paragraph below?

> *He got up, tears streaming down his cheek. Him, the tough guy, crying. Who would have believed it?*
>
> *He took his leather jacket (the one I'd bought him) from the back of the chair, but it snagged on the edge of the table and the contents of a pocket spilled out. His mobile phone fell to the floor, but there was something else, a small, black box. The sort you get from a jewellers.*

❸ Add two lines of dialogue: one from the **narrator**, one from her boyfriend.

STRUCTURING NARRATIVES

If you are asked to write a full story, how should the **narrative arc** be structured? Here is a possible plan based on the photo on page 61.

Stage	Details
Exposition: *introducing the situation, setting etc.*	Boy meets girl at their usual café. She plans to tell him something important.
Rising action; *the story develops, complications arise*	He realises something is wrong; she is not her usual self.
Climax: *the moment of most drama or emotion*	She breaks up with him, and he gets up to leave. A box with a ring falls to the floor.
Falling action: *tension drops but things are not yet resolved*	She apologises, but it's too late. He leaves, without the box/ring. She picks up the ring.
Resolution: *things are uncovered, explained or resolved – not always happily*	She goes round to his flat. He has moved out. There is a note …

❹ Think of a good ending. Could the note reveal something surprising?

Remember the **complication** – there would not be a story without a 'problem'. It can be humorous or serious – but something must 'break the flow'.

THE IMPORTANCE OF LOCATION

For short stories, or extracts from them, it is best to stick to one or two main locations. For example, from the story above – the café and the flat. Unless a location is central to the story (for example, a story about being stuck in a cave), then a few lines or details about setting them will suffice:

> *Ella made her way past the small oval tables and the counter with the sticky buns and lukewarm sausage rolls.*

> *Joe's room was sparse and smelt of bleach. The shelves were empty and the bed had been stripped. A single light bulb dangled from the ceiling…*

❺ Read this story task:

Write a story in which someone is placed in an awkward situation. The story can be real or imagined.

a) First generate ideas using a spider diagram. Copy and complete this one or create one of your own.

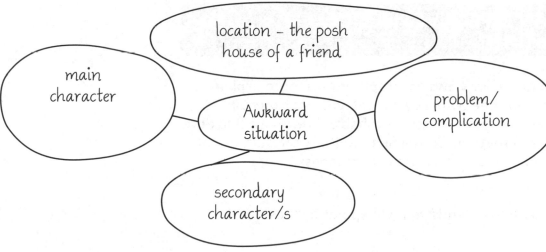

b) Add as many further details as you can to your diagram. For example, for 'location':

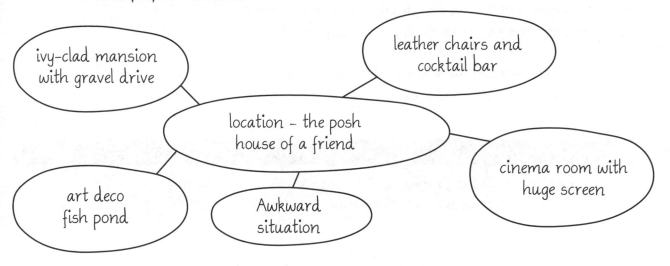

c) Then, use the five stages of the story to create your structure, as follows:

| Exposition | → | Rising action | → | Climax | → | Falling action | → | Resolution |

APPLYING YOUR SKILLS   A05 A06

❻ Write a story which begins with someone losing something important or valuable.

Remember:

● Before you start writing, generate ideas using a diagram or list as shown.

● Turn your ideas into a clear plan of five stages with a main character.

● Make your opening interesting: don't waste time on too many facts/much information.

● Maintain a clear voice and perspective for your main character (first or third person).

● Use visual details to make your story memorable.

4.9 WRITING TO EXPRESS A PERSONAL VIEWPOINT

Many of the skills you have learned about also apply to writing tasks when you are asked to express a particular view, but there are some specific ones worth using.

WHAT MAKES AN EFFECTIVE PIECE OF VIEWPOINT WRITING?

When you are asked to give your views on a topic or idea, or to explain how much you agree or disagree with a statement, you are expressing a viewpoint or an opinion. It is something you probably do without thinking every day, but in an exam situation you will need to think carefully about your choice of words and how you structure your response.

Effective viewpoint writing should:

- Ensure the reader **fully understands your viewpoint** by the end of the text
- Use the most suitable **register** and **style** for the **form, purpose** and **audience**
- Have a **consistent argument**, that is **sustained** throughout the text
- Use a range of **appropriate evidence** or **points** to support the overall view
- Use a range of **persuasive techniques** appropriate to the task
- **End strongly** in order to make sure the reader is persuaded by your argument

EXAM FOCUS

Read how one student has planned a response for this task. Note how she has highlighted and annotated the key words in the task.

Establishes the reader/audience

Signals the purpose and content

Your school's head teacher has asked students to submit ideas for ways in which the health and well-being of students can be improved. Write a letter to him/her proposing ideas which you believe will help.

Identifies the form or type of text

You could include:

- examples of changes that could be made to the school environment
- ideas to persuade students to exercise more and eat healthily.

❶ What ideas do you have? Use a spider diagram like the one on page 63 to jot down as many ideas as possible in a minute. Refer to the two bullets at the end of the task to help you.

REGISTER AND STYLE

Knowing who you are writing for (reader/audience), and the form (letter), will influence the **register** and **style** of your response.

EXAM FOCUS

Here is the opening to the task written by the same student.

> **Uses suitably formal tone/style**

> Dear Mrs Stockdale,
>
> As you requested, I am writing to provide some ideas to improve the general physical and mental health of students. I believe the ideas I am offering will make a significant change to the school, and all who spend time here.

> **Neatly paraphrases the task wording which includes 'well-being' not just physical 'wellness'**

> **Makes it clear that physical health will be addressed first with this topic sentence**

> Firstly, I want to address the issue of physical health. Studies have shown that it is important to get the heart rate up, and the best way of doing that is exercise. Unfortunately, the school fields are completely unusable for much of the Autumn and Spring terms: they are muddy, soaked and dangerously bumpy, so my main proposal is to create more all weather pitches for football, netball, hockey, and so on...

> **Provides evidence or background support for point**

> **Uses similar wording ('proposal') to the task to introduce the key idea clearly**

❷ What specific evidence does the student use to support the idea of 'all-weather pitches'?

❸ What strong **adverb-adjective** combinations does she use to describe the state of the school playing-fields in the second paragraph?

❹ What **pattern of three** adjectives is used to describe the pitches? What effect is created?

TOP TIP

Adverb-adjective combinations are often used to express strong feelings as writers use **intensifiers** to make an argument more powerful. For example, '*totally* unacceptable', '*utterly* wrong', '*incredibly* foolish'.

❺ Copy and complete the next paragraph in the same response, selecting the most apt words from each set of options. Retain the polite, formal style but choose appropriate intensifiers where needed.

*A second **idea/thing/suggestion** I have come up with is to create a quiet zone where **kids/students/children** can go to **unwind/chillax/chill out**. Life at school can be **incredibly/partly/rather** busy and **super/hugely** challenging. Of course, someone would need to **keep an eye on/check out/monitor** behaviour but that should not prove too difficult.*

PLANNING A VIEWPOINT ESSAY

A number of structures can be used or adapted in a viewpoint essay.

Structure	Explanation	Good because...	But think about...
Simple 'for' paragraphs	Each paragraph has at least one suggestion, idea or point which you believe is right.	Very clear – your views will be easy to follow.	... including at least one paragraph with opposing views for balance
'For' and 'against' paragraphs	Alternate paragraphs give one side and then the other in turn.	The other view is included – sounds balanced.	... stressing *your* viewpoint in the conclusion
Paragraphs include both 'for/against' at same time.	Each paragraph deals with one idea or point, but includes the opposing argument too.	The opposing argument can be 'knocked down' each time.	... not over-complicating things. The odd paragraph without a counter-argument is fine!
A mix of all of these!	You sometimes have one paragraph for a key idea, then a second where you mix 'for/against'....and so on.	You show subtle control over your ideas and how to adapt your writing.	... using your 'for' paragraph as a starting point, then 'mixed' paragraphs after that

❻ Which would you choose? Is there one that would suit your way of writing?

❼ Look back at the letter on the last page – which one (or ones) of these structures do you think the writer is following?

APPLYING YOUR SKILLS   (A05) (A06)

❽ Now, read and complete this task.

'We must use the countryside to build new housing estates – everyone needs somewhere to live!'

Write a speech to be given to local people in which you argue for or against this statement.

Remember:

- Before you start writing, generate ideas using a spider diagram or list.
- Turn your ideas into a clear plan based on one of the options in the table on page 66.
- Make sure you support your views with evidence.
- Use language techniques from earlier in this chapter to influence your listeners.

PROGRESS CHECK FOR CHAPTER FOUR   ✓

GOOD PROGRESS

I can:

- Use a good range of vocabulary ☐
- Use a range of different sentences appropriately ☐
- Punctuate accurately, observing the main rules and conventions ☐
- Understand the different functions of paragraphs and use connectives to make meaning clear ☐
- Understand the different effects created by a range of language devices and techniques and can apply some of them to my descriptive, narrative and viewpoint writing ☐

EXCELLENT PROGRESS

I can:

- Use vocabulary in a precise and vivid way ☐
- Use and adapt a wide range of sentences with a clear impact in mind ☐
- Punctuate accurately but also adapt punctuation for creative impact ☐
- Select and structure my paragraphs in a range of ways, and use a variety of connectives for meaning and effect ☐
- Select from a rich and varied range of language devices and techniques to create original and thoughtful descriptive, narrative and viewpoint writing ☐

5.1 INTRODUCTION TO SAMPLE TASKS

In this section of the book, you will have a chance to complete three tasks which are similar, if not identical, to the writing tasks you will encounter in your GCSE English Language and English Literature exams.

For each one, follow **the four stages** suggested and then use the grid below to evaluate your answers. The criteria will vary according to what exam board you are following and the type of task, but here are some broad guidelines:

TYPICAL FEATURES OF MID-LEVEL AND HIGH-LEVEL RESPONSES

GCSE	Mid-level response	High-level response
English Language	*Clear, generally accurate. Usually engaging/interesting*	*Compelling and convincing ideas and expression*
Content	Generally well-matched to the task, audience and purpose. Interesting for the reader.	Extremely well matched to the task, audience and purpose. Convincing ideas and highly engaging for reader.
Language	Language and vocabulary clearly chosen for effect on reader. Clear paragraphs which are linked effectively, using some structural devices (e.g. connectives).	Wide range of language devices and ambitious vocabulary which sustains impact through whole text. Varied and inventive use of structure e.g. organisation of ideas, paragraphing, etc.
SPaG	Generally accurate spelling and use of a variety of sentence forms. Range of punctuation used, usually correctly.	Consistently accurate spelling and wide range of sentence forms for effect Wide range of punctuation used for impact.
English Literature	*Shows clear understanding*	*Convincing, critical analysis*
Content	Range of appropriate text references and evidence.	Precise text references and evidence selected as best to use.
Language	Ideas explained clearly with relevant terminology (e.g. rhyme) used.	Texts analysed with overall sense of task with very well-chosen terminology used.
SPaG	Reasonable range of vocabulary, sentence structures and generally accurate spelling and punctuation.	Wide range of vocabulary, and consistent accuracy of sentences, spelling and punctuation.

Once you have completed each task and the evaluation, check the 'Answers' section on pages 79-84 to see student responses at two different levels – 'Mid' and 'High' – with tips for improvement. How do your answers compare?

5.2 TASK A: CREATIVE WRITING – MAKING AN IMPACT

INTRODUCTION

For this task, you will need to draw on key descriptive and narrative skills. If you need to, check back to 4.7 and 4.8, as well as appropriate language units (e.g. 4.1 on vocabulary), before you start.

First, read the following task carefully. Then, before you begin, check the section entitled 'How to approach the task' on page 70.

YOUR TASK

> You have been asked to provide a piece of creative writing about children discovering secret places.
>
> Write a story set in a hidden place as suggested by this picture.

TOP TIP

The 40 marks allowed here include **24 marks** for content and organisation and **16 marks** for technical accuracy. If you wish to time yourself for exam practice, allow yourself **45 minutes** or so.

[40 marks]

HOW TO APPROACH THE TASK

Follow stages one to four below to help you generate ideas, plan and write your response to the task.

Stage one: quickly underline the key words in the story title/task.

Stage two: generate ideas for your story by noting down ideas, a key character, setting etc. You can refer back to 2.1, 2.2 and 4.8 for ideas, if you wish. Remember the five point narrative arc.

Stage three: write your story.

Remember:

- Engage the reader's interest immediately.
- Stick to one main character and **plot**.
- Consider the part (if any) dialogue could play.
- Structure your story carefully, using consistent tenses.
- Check SPaG as you go along, watching out especially for the comma splice, and other simple punctuation errors.

Stage four: do a final proof-read at the end. At this stage, don't make messy changes that will make your story impossible to read, but do correct any small, obvious errors. Cross out the mistake with a single line and write in the correction (if needed).

5.3 TASK B: NON-FICTION WRITING – EXPRESSING A POINT OF VIEW

INTRODUCTION

For this task, you will need to draw on key persuasive or argumentative skills. If you need to, refer back to 4.9, as well as appropriate to language units (e.g. 4.5 on connectives), before you start.

First, read the following task carefully. Then, before you begin, check the section entitled 'How to approach the task' under the task itself.

YOUR TASK

> 'The popularity of the "selfie" shows how vain we have all become. Rather than looking at ourselves, we should be taking note of what is going on around us.'
>
> Write a blog for a website read by people your own age in which you express your views on this issue.

[40 marks]

TOP TIP

The 40 marks allowed here include **24 marks** for content and organisation and **16 marks** for technical accuracy. If you wish to time yourself for exam practice, allow yourself **45 minutes** or so.

HOW TO APPROACH THE TASK

Stage one: underline the key words in the task, e.g. form, purpose and audience.

Stage two: quickly jot down ideas for/against the viewpoint, and decide on your own opinion. You can check back to 2.1, 2.2 and 4.9 for ideas, if you wish. Then, decide how you will organise your points. (Look again at the table in 4.9 on page 66.)

Stage three: write your article.

Remember:

- Use the right register for the form/audience.
- Make sure your viewpoint is clear, throughout and at the end.
- Consider how you can use emotive or persuasive language.
- Structure your article in a way you are comfortable with.
- Check SPaG as you go along, watching out especially for the comma splice, and other simple punctuation errors.

Stage four: do a final proof-read at the end. At this stage, don't make messy changes that will make your story impossible to read, but do correct any small, obvious errors. Cross out the mistake with a single line and write in the correction (if needed).

5.4 TASK C: UNSEEN POETRY – ANALYSING A WRITER'S METHODS

INTRODUCTION

For this task, you will need to draw on key analysis skills and how these can be demonstrated in your writing. If you need to, check back to 3.4, as well as appropriate language units (e.g. 1.5 on quoting effectively), before you start.

First, read the following task carefully. Then, before you begin, check the section entitled 'How to approach the task' on page 73.

YOUR TASK

> How does the poet present the speaker's feelings about the woman he loved?

[24 marks]

TOP TIP

If you wish to time yourself for exam practice, allow yourself **35 minutes** or so.

THE POEM

Beeny Cliff

O the opal and the sapphire of that wandering western sea,
And the woman riding high above with bright hair flapping free –
The woman whom I loved so, and who loyally loved me.

The pale mews[1] plained below us, and the waves seemed far away
5 In a nether[2] sky, engrossed in saying their ceaseless babbling say,
As we laughed light-heartedly aloft on that clear-sunned March day.

A little cloud then cloaked us, and there flew an irised[3] rain,
And the Atlantic dyed its levels with a dull misfeatured stain,
And then the sun burst out again, and purples prinked[4] the main[5].

10 – Still in all its chasmal beauty bulks old Beeny to the sky,
And shall she and I not go there once again now March is nigh,
And the sweet things said in that March say anew there by and by?

What if still in chasmal beauty looms that wild weird western shore,
The woman now is – elsewhere – whom the ambling pony bore,
15 And nor knows nor cares for Beeny, and will laugh there nevermore.

Thomas Hardy

Glossary:
[1] *mews* – gulls
[2] *nether* – low
[3] *irised* – like the iris (blue/violet flower)
[4] *prinked* – adorned or decorated with
[5] *main* – the sea

HOW TO APPROACH THE TASK

Follow stages one to four below to help you generate ideas, plan and write your response to the task.

Stage one: read the poem through once without making notes.

Stage two: re-read and annotate the poem in the light of the question by:

- Highlighting powerful or key words/phrases
- Noting down questions, ideas, observations
- Highlighting structural elements related to the sound, sequence and rhythm of the poem
- Summing up the 'story' told

Stage three: decide the sequence for your response (e.g. work through the poem section by section) and write your response.

Remember:

- Quote selectively.
- Explain the writer's methods and their effects.
- Check SPaG as you go along, watching out especially for the comma splice, and other simple punctuation errors that might make your analysis less clear or fluent.

Stage four: do a final proof-read at the end. At this stage, don't make messy changes that will make your story impossible to read, but do correct any small, obvious errors. Cross out the mistake with a single line and write in the correction (if needed).

ANSWERS

CHAPTER ONE

1.1 Writing in both GCSE English Language and Literature [pp. 5–7]

1 AO4 (English Literature) and AO6 (English Language) are identical, because accuracy in spelling, punctuation and grammar is assessed in both subjects.

2 This will depend on the subjects you study but you might have to write short factual answers in Science, or Languages; longer essays in History, Geography or Religious Studies.

3 Possible answer for A: 2-3 paragraphs; 6-10 marks.

Possible answer for B: 5-6 paras (full-length essay); 25-30 marks.

1.2 Task, audience and purpose [pp. 8–9]

1 Main purpose: to persuade the reader that charity shops can improve a run-down high street.

2 Secondary purpose: to describe (what the street looks like); to explain (the change since the charity shops arrived).

3 Student uses: personal pronouns 'our' 'us'; mentions 'the school' (doesn't mention its name so it is clear she expects listeners to share same knowledge);

Persuasive features: statement of opinion: 'I strongly believe'; powerful images: 'eat up our money'; negative adjective 'harmful'.

4 Possible completed paragraph: *It would be wonderful to have a moment free of the poisonous fumes and thundering noise of motorbikes, cars and lorries. Our town deserves better and we can surely press for at least one weekend a month when we can hear the birds singing and the children playing outdoors.*

1.3 Forms of writing [pp. 10–11]

1 Most likely answers: A = original story, possibly newspaper report; B = diary, letter, email; possibly blog or story; C = speech, letter, blog, email, newspaper article; possibly diary.

2 Opinion: people should not be allowed to own too many pets!

3 Story: might be very similar, but perhaps more focus on character and 'plot' and would not end with a rhetorical question. Diary: likely to refer to events that have just happened rather than a few days ago.

4 Answers will vary, but subjects requiring critical writing like this, such as History or Religious Studies, will be included.

5 Answers will vary.

1.4 Creating an impact [pp. 12–13]

1 Effects created by: Student A = b), c), d), f); Student B = a), e); Student C = a), d), e.

2 Changes introduced in the extract: a), b), d), e), i).

3 Answers will vary.

1.5 Using quotations effectively [pp. 14–15]

1 Possible rewritten sentence: *Scrooge describes how he is 'merry as a school boy' and 'giddy as a drunken man', emphasising how joyful he is.* Or *Dickens emphasises how joyful Scrooge is when he describes him as 'merry as a school boy' and 'giddy as a drunken man.'*

2 The evidence comes at the start of the paragraph with the use of the quotation.

3 The final sentence adds an explanation of what emotions are 'manufactured', i.e. being in love with the idea of love.

4 Answers will vary.

1.6 Spelling, punctuation and grammar [pp. 16–21]

1 Answers will vary.

2 Answers will vary.

3 Answers will vary.

5ator" il

. izable

CHAPTER TWO

2.1 Generating ideas [pp. 22–4]

1 Other key words or phrases: 'parents' worries about safety' [content], 'article', 'school magazine', [form] 'persuade……..become more active' [purpose] 'fellow students' [audience].

2 Two annotations on left; 'Keeping up with social media..' and 'No need for green spaces'.

3. **Possible points:** 'health is as much a safety concern as letting children play'; 'active lives are good for your physical health, diet etc.', 'also good for mental well-being'; 'good for team-building and other social skills', 'fun!' etc.

4. Answers will vary.

5. Answers will vary.

6. Highlighted key words from which to generate ideas: A proposal has been made to close the local ten-pin bowling alley and replace it with a discount shop. Write an article for your local paper to share your views on this proposal. You could write in favour or against this proposal.

Possible arguments: For proposal – too expensive, no one goes, not popular compared with other activities, too many issues with teenagers causing problems; sells fast food and cold drinks at high prices; discount store will help families looking for a bargain; create jobs.

Against proposal – one less thing for young people to do; good for families; good for parties; suitable for all abilities; discount shop will create parking problems; sells poor quality goods.

2.2 Effective planning [pp. 25–7]

1 Answers will vary.

2 Exposition = a); Rising Action = b); Climax = e); Falling action = d) Resolution = c)

3 Starting with the most dramatic event would grab the reader's attention, raise questions about why Jools is in that situation, who the people who are trying to find her etc. – the background can be filled in later.

4 He/she has structured by ideas by jumping from the opening to the end of the poem to make a point.

5 **Possible structures:** deal with various aspects like language, structure etc. one at a time; work through the poem verse by verse; deal with key ideas/points related to the meaning/focus of the task.

6 **Possible points for viewpoint essay:** For – no danger of road vehicles and bikes coming into collision; protection for cyclists; cyclists do not use the road properly and cannot be seen by lorries; encourage councils to think about other road calming/eco measures;

Against – cyclists have as much right as other road users; many roads do not have cycle lanes; riding on the pavement is very dangerous to pedestrians especially children; even cycle lanes are sometimes used by other vehicles, illegally.

CHAPTER THREE

3.1 Writing effective short and longer answers [pp. 28–9]

1 a) Paraphrase: *A stranger might have been struck by the crockery being thrown around, or knocked over by the children racing out of the kitchen.*

Quotation: *Because the children were 'catapulting their dishes'; or the stranger might have been 'trampled' as the children left the kitchen.*

b) Paraphrase: *Joseph's family were lucky in that they had food and were able to attend school.*

Quotation: Joseph's family were lucky to have food 'albeit meagre' and 'they did make it to school' at least.

2 **Possible evaluation of the response:** *It tackles the writer's use of words and phrases. It does analyse, to a point, explaining the effect of the adjectives. These points might have been developed further, perhaps. It has a conclusion which sums up the overall impression of Joseph's life.*

3 **Possible paragraph on short sentence forms:** *The writer uses short sentences for emphasis and to sum up ideas. The exclamation 'How awful it was!' follows the longer sentence detailing how 'invisible' Joseph felt and stresses the impact on him. The final sentence 'Life was tough' effectively sums up the detailed account of the family's poor clothing and sanitary facilities.*

3.2 Writing about fiction texts [pp. 30–1]

1 Answers will vary.

2 *As the novel* <u>opens</u>, *Orwell* <u>creates</u> *a picture of a farm that is poorly run, and* <u>describes</u> *an owner, Mr Jone,s who is lazy and ill-tempered. As the* <u>initial</u> *events* <u>unfold</u>, *we see the emergence of characters who will have significant impact on the* <u>narrative</u>.

3 Answers will vary.

3.3 Writing about non-fiction texts [pp. 32–3]

1 Student A

2 Student B

3 Student B uses a wider range of verbs – such as 'implies', 'states', 'suggests' etc.

4 Student B – the letter writer's feelings of frustration and fascination are well explained and evidenced.

5 **Possible rewritten paragraph:** *The writer* <u>states</u> *that smartphones 'distract' him from 'living' and he* <u>complains</u> *they are like 'a constant child that needs attention.' This* <u>suggests</u> *that he feels responsibility but also* <u>implies</u> *that they are a source of irritation.*

3.4 Writing about poetry and drama [pp. 34–5]

1 Answers will vary.

2 Answers will vary.

3 Answers will vary.

4 **Possible answer:** *The final sentence introduces the idea of 'perspective' – and how the poem now focuses on a different voice/character in the poem.*

5 Answers will vary.

3.5 Selecting and synthesising information [pp. 36–37]

1 Text A: 'strange' mass of people /sobbed 'hysterically'/made 'convulsive groans'/gave 'shrieks and screams'/ spoke with' hoarse', 'overstrained voices'/clapped hands 'violently'.

Text B: 'anxiety' of crowd/'murmuring wave of discontent'/'bit...fingernails'/'gasped'/'hid their faces'/ seemed 'terrified'.

2 **Possible comparative paragraph:** *Both crowds seem to have lost control of their senses, to a degree. The revival group seem overcome with emotion which pours out of them with 'sobbing', 'groans' and 'shrieks', while the football crowd seem racked with nerves as they bite 'their fingernails and hide their faces.*

3 Answers will vary.

3.6 Comparing and contrasting [pp. 38–41]

1 Answers will vary.

2 **Annotated paragraph:** <u>*Scrooge's transformation is very gradual over the course of the novel.*</u> [**topic sentence**] <u>*At first*</u> [**time marker**], *he is emotionally affected by seeing scenes from his past life for example when he 'wept to see his poor forgotten self'.* <u>*However*</u> [**connective**], *by the end he is making a pledge to change his actions, not just how he feels, claiming he is 'not the man' he once was.*

3 **Possible comparative paragraph:** *Both poems explore Autumn and reflect on nature to suggest mood. In 'To Autumn' Keats creates a warm glow through noun phrases such as 'mellow fruitfulness' and 'maturing sun', almost like the way a fine wine or cheese matures. In contrast, in 'Autumn Song', Rossetti conveys a sense of decay and decline, in particular by rhyming 'fall of the leaf' with 'grief'.*

4 Answers will vary.

5 a) whereas/while/although; b) both; c) yet/however/ although/but

6 Answers will vary.

CHAPTER FOUR

4.1 Vocabulary for impact [pp. 42–3]

1 It is Paolo who is dancing – he is the writer's 'best-friend'. He was 'jiggling … like a fish on a line.' Giovanna is the writer's sister – she sings along loudly to her 'favourite song.' The food on the table is listed.

2 *Who* was singing and dancing (Paolo, Giovanna); *how* they were doing it (e.g. 'like a fish on a line'); *what* specific food was eaten (e.g. foccacia).

3 **Suggested response:** *Suddenly there was a huge* <u>bang</u>. *With all the dancing, a* <u>wardrobe</u> *had* <u>toppled</u> *over and* <u>slammed</u> *onto the floor. My father* <u>rushed</u> *into the room. 'What's going on?' he* <u>demanded</u>, *angrily.*

4 Answers will vary.

[78]

5 Synonym groups could be: *hot, spicy, tangy; acidic, bitter* and *juicy, fresh, luscious.*

You could argue that some of these are not direct synonyms – for example something 'juicy' isn't always 'fresh' but it is likely to be!

6 Answers will vary.

7 Most positive adjectives: *talkative; chatty; communicative;* most negative adjectives: *loud-mouthed; gossipy; verbose*

8 and **9** Answers to both will vary.

4.2 Sentences for variety and effect [pp. 44–5]

1 The short sentences echo the short, precise movements the safe-breaker is making and the excitement/tension as the combination is broken.

2 The minor sentences are: 'First, a few notches to the right'; 'Listened'; 'Another click'. 'Listened closely', 'Click'. 'Yes!'

You could argue that the words 'Click' and 'Yes' are really utterances rather than sentences, but they do stand for omitted words (e.g. 'Yes' = 'Yes, I had managed it').

3 Answers will vary.

4 Re-written paragraph: *We must look at ourselves. Each day we make decisions about where we buy products and we make choices about what we eat. Yet despite warnings from health professionals about diabetes and heart disease, we continue to disregard our own bodies.*

5 **Active and passive headlines:** A '<u>Junk food</u> destroys young lives' = active – emphasis is on the underlined subject; B '<u>Young lives</u> destroyed by junk food' = passive, emphasis on the first two words; C '<u>Young lives</u> destroyed' = passive; emphasis solely on underlined words.

6 The effect of omitting the 'do-er' is to place the emphasis entirely on what has happened not the cause (which is completely absent).

7 Answers will vary.

4.3 Punctuation for clarity and creativity [pp. 46–7]

1 Full-stop has been added at end of first sentence – the key point. A comma has been added to separate actions in list.

2 A colon could have been used instead of the first full-stop.

3 First two questions are used rhetorically. Final question is more exploratory – setting up debate and looking back to previous questions.

4 **Possible paragraph:** *Should I just accept that she wasn't going to come? Why not pay for my coffee and just leave? But it's only been 10 minutes so am I being fair, I wonder?*

5 Brackets are used to provide brief evidence of each quotation without breaking the flow of the sentence as a whole.

6 Answers will vary.

7 A question mark has been used in the second paragraph to signal a rhetorical question. A colon has been used to introduce what can be seen when writer looks down.

8 Answers will vary.

4.4 Paragraphs for organisation and sequence [pp. 48–9]

1 The first paragraph introduces new characters; the second changes the time and introduces a specific location; also, its tone is lighter, less dramatic.

2 The story could begin with paragraphs 2 and 3. If starting with '2', then the tension hanging over the fact we know the writer was to blame would be lost, but there would be more of a surprise element later. If beginning with '3', the story would begin with action and drama, which might engage the reader straight away.

3 Paragraph 4 could involve the boys leaving with the tree but then Dev gets stuck in the back door.

In Paragraph 5, the school caretaker could catch Dev while the narrator abandons him and runs off …

4 **Possible arguments for team sports:** *cool kit; learn responsibility; teaches you how to win/lose gracefully; healthy activity*

5 Answers will vary.

4.5 Connectives for cohesion [pp. 50–1]

1 Answers will vary.

2 **Possible completed paragraph:** <u>Both</u> *cycling and driving cars can be dangerous activities.* <u>However/Yet,</u> *it is clear that if you are on a bike, you have less protection* <u>than</u> *car drivers. There is also the matter of visibility.* <u>On the one hand,</u> *cars have multiple mirrors,* <u>whereas</u> *bikes have none or very few.*

3 **Possible completed paragraph:** *I want to talk to you about fitness.* <u>Because</u> *of Laura Trott's success, I took up cycling.* <u>As a result</u> *I am now a regular member of my cycling team.* <u>If</u> *you take it up, you* <u>may/might/will</u> *enjoy it just as much as I do.*

4 Answers will vary.

4.6 Simile, metaphor and other language techniques [pp. 52–5]

1 **Possible similes and metaphors:** *The curving river sparkled* <u>like a twisted chain of silver</u>.

Tiny leaping fish were <u>darting arrows.</u> The sun's rays <u>smiled on us</u>.

A narrow, pointed boat <u>sliced through</u> the water <u>like a thin dagger</u>.

2 Possible analogy: *The pulse throbs <u>like an electric generator, or a low rhythmic motor</u> in the background.*

3 Possible answer: *She opened the bedroom door. On the floor, an abandoned <u>coffee cup</u> lay on its side. On the unmade bed, the pillow still showed the imprint of <u>a half-turned face</u>. The window was half-open and outside on the tree she could see <u>a single, tiny sparrow shivering in the cold</u>.*

4 The litter has been personified as if it were an invading or occupying force.

5 Answers will vary.

6 Completed paragraph: *The kettle <u>hissed</u> as the steam burst out, and old Ma Smith tottered across the floor slowly, <u>gasping</u> for breath as she did so. By the time she got to the old stove, the water had boiled dry and when she lifted the spout, only a tiny <u>dribble</u> came out. Outside in the yard, a hen <u>clucked</u> in its repetitive way, and the little stream by the gate <u>gurgled</u> happily.*

7 Answers will vary.

4.7 Writing a descriptive text [pp. 56–60]

1 Student A's is the most effective description because it builds up tension and atmosphere though carefully chosen language which 'shows' the reader rather than 'telling' them.

2 Student B's is less effective because it lacks close, detailed description and specific vocabulary.

3 Successful descriptive features: strong sensory imagery – appeal to sight, touch; detailed, precise vocabulary – 'frozen waters', 'icy locks', 'skeletal spiders'; varied sentences lengths/types for impact.

4 Answers will vary.

5 Answers will vary.

6 Other imagined detail: the 'distant sun'

7 and **8** Answers to both will vary.

9 Answers will vary.

10 Answers will vary.

4.8 Writing a narrative or short story [pp. 61–3]

1 B is more likely to grab the reader's attention as it:

- Immerses the reader in the dangerous situation
- Focuses on one main character and uses their perspective
- Plunges straight into the action, showing what's going on.
- Uses vivid descriptive detail, e.g. 'The ball... like a red bullet'.

2 Extract C best fits the image – the girl, Ellie, is trying to impress on her boyfriend that it's over and the story reflects her perspective even though it is written in the third person.

Voice A is the first-person narrative of the boyfriend; voice B is the third-person narrative from the café manager's viewpoint; voice D is the first-person narrative of an older customer in the café.

3 and **4** Answers to both will vary.

5, 6 and **7** Answers to all three will vary.

4.9 Writing to express a personal viewpoint [pp. 64–7]

1 Answers will vary.

2 Specific evidence to support all-weather pitches: the student says 'the school fields are completely unusable for much of the Autumn and Spring terms'

3 Adverb-adjective combinations: 'completely unusable'; 'dangerously bumpy'

4 Pattern of three: 'they are muddy, soaked and dangerously bumpy'

5 Completed paragraph: *A second <u>suggestion</u> I have come up with is to create a quiet zone where <u>students</u> can go to <u>unwind</u>. Life at school can be <u>incredibly</u> busy and <u>extremely</u> challenging. Of course, someone would need to <u>monitor</u> behaviour but that should not prove too difficult.*

6 Answers will vary.

7 Essay structure followed in letter: Simple 'for' paragraphs, although you would need to see the whole essay to be sure.

8 Answers will vary.

CHAPTER FIVE

5.1 Introduction to the sample tasks [p. 68]

No answers required.

5.2 Task A: Creative writing – making an impact [pp. 69–70]

Student A: extract from a Mid Level response

Effective opening paragraph establishes setting

I didn't believe Josie was telling the truth until I saw it for myself – the huge, abandoned mansion in the forest. But when we walked through the thick trees and into the open field where it was, I knew she wasn't lying.

'It's our secret place,' she said.

We were seven years old and twins and we did everything together. Our family lived on the edge of the big forest and our dad was a woodcutter. Our mother was a nurse and worked nights, so we didn't see her much.

Clear characterisation and 'filling in' background

Good use of dialogue to build characterisation

'Dad will wonder where we've got to,' I said. I wasn't very adventurous, not like Josie.

'No he won't,' she replied. 'Anyway, he's working on the other side of the forest.'

She walked up to the walls of the mansion. There was wet, green ivy growing around the bottom. Like a slimy monster that was ready to grab us. All the windows were empty with no glass left. The place gave me the creeps if I'm honest.

Attempt at using imagery

'Don't go in!' I warned her, but as usual she didn't listen.

She pushed on the big oak door. I don't think she expected it to open but it did. It gave a groan and swung open. I saw her standing there looking in but I was too afraid to move.

Use of short sentences for dramatic impact

Then it happened. She took a step forward and disappeared! There was no sound, just the sight of her going into the blackness, like she'd fallen into a black hole in space.

I rushed forward, calling out her name but she didn't answer. When I got to the entrance I stared in. It gave me a terrible shock because there was no floor, just a gaping great space. I couldn't see anything in the gloom but I knew it wasn't good. All I could think of was needing to find our father, so I turned and ran.

The path was long and winding, and sometimes I had to jump over fallen logs and twisted branches. Hurry, I told myself. Josie might not have much time! The tall trees seemed to be like enemies, trying to prevent my progress. Then it was getting dark, and I felt like I'd lost my way. Surely it was too late. I couldn't save Josie now. But then, just as I thought I wouldn't find my father, I saw a light in the woods. At last!

Effective, if rather basic, description

Good use of varied sentence structures to build suspense

Comment

A clearly structured story with some effective characterisation. The visual details could perhaps be a little more striking and original, and a slightly wider vocabulary would help (note the repetition of 'space') but overall this engages the reader's interest.

Student B: extract from a High Level response

Opening sentence immediately draws reader in	I shouldn't have followed them, but I did. It was easy really. They were a gang, talking, laughing amongst themselves, making fun of others. Bullying, sometimes. I was small, an outsider so no one noticed me. They didn't notice me.

I knew they had a secret place in the woods as after school rather than catch the bus like everyone else, they leapt on their bikes and disappeared along the narrow, stony path which led along the canal, over the hump-backed bridge and into 'The Wilderness'. That was what everyone called it, but it was really just a wood on the edge of town. Not pretty – full of stunted birches and black crows that stared down at you or cackled like witches as you passed.

Concise, vivid details using noun phrases

Apt simile for the setting

Excellent use of specific vocabulary to create mood

I didn't have a bike, but as soon as they were out of sight I ran breathlessly along the canal path and followed the snaking muddy track in the wood. I could just about hear their voices ahead, laughs and cries echoing off the walls of trees and twisted roots.

New paragraph moves story along

It got gloomy quickly, and soon I had my mobile phone's light on, its thin beam like a white splinter splitting the darkness ahead of me. Now it was quiet. The voices gone. Even the crows were silent. I was in the middle of 'The Wilderness' with no idea where I was. I looked down and even the muddy track had disappeared. I was standing on soft, mossy grass, and behind me I could see the imprints of my school shoes slowly vanishing as the moss sprang back into place.

Focusing in on visual detail for effect

Then, out of nowhere, an icy hand was on my wrist and I was pulled violently to one side.

One-sentence paragraph creates drama

Dialogue creates sense of mystery

'Don't breathe a say a word,' a voice said. A girl's voice. It had an accent, as if from an exotic country. I could smell incense, or something. Then I heard a match being struck. A light flared and I could see I was in front of a huge, stone edifice.

It was a temple – or had been once. How did it get here? And who was the girl?

Narrator's questions echo what reader is thinking

Comment

This is a compellingly told story which engages the interest from the start. Characterisation and the dialogue is effective and description is vivid and detailed, creating a convincing mood and atmosphere. The structure is handled very well, and there is excellent variety of sentence and paragraph styles to create impact.

5.3 Task A: Non-fiction writing – expressing a point of view [p. 71]

Sample A: Mid Level response

Establishes clear opinion straight away	*Okay – I admit that I am a big fan of the 'selfie.' Whenever I have the chance to snap my face at a party or when I'm out with my mates, I take it. Like everyone else, I post it on social media and check to see how many 'likes' I get. For me it's natural, I guess.*

Informal usage but probably acceptable in a blog

Topic sentence signals new paragraph focus

I don't really think it is about how vain I am though. Let's face it, if you saw some of the photos I post of myself, you would not say I'm vain! There are some that are dead embarrassing, like when I have tomato ketchup on my chin, or my hair is all messed up. I look really awful, but I still take the 'selfie'. I suppose it's saying 'this is me' – take me as I am.

Visual detail supports point

Pattern of three followed by short emphatic sentence

Of course I know some people do use them to show off. They wait till their hair is perfect. They adjust how they are standing, where they are looking or the angle of their heads. It's madness. Maybe they are hoping a model agency or Hollywood will notice them by chance and offer them a career there and then. I don't know, but life's too short to wait until you're looking perfect.

Introduces a counter argument

I don't see what is wrong with selfies at famous places or beauty spots. It's basically like a diary recording where you were and when. Something you can look at again later and say to yourself – did I really go there? Like you see people in front of the Taj Mahal or at the top of the Eiffel Tower. Is it so different from buying a postcard or getting someone else to take a pic of you?

Good use of rhetorical question

Makes shift to new point but rather suddenly

Anyway, the people I know do take notice of their surroundings when they take a selfie. In fact, I'd say they were even more aware of what's around them. I think they're harmless, and I for one will continue taking them.

Clear restatement of viewpoint

Comment

This is a simply argued piece that makes the writer's viewpoint clear. Paragraphs are used to establish his viewpoint through a range of different points, and there is one attempt to tackle counter-arguments. Some persuasive devices are used, but the article perhaps ends rather abruptly by starting a new point about 'noticing surroundings' which could be developed before concluding to give a slightly longer, more rounded response.

Sample B: High Level response

Opening paragraph opens up the debate skillfully through verbal patterning and questions

It's clear that the 'selfie' is a big, big part of all our lives. Wherever we are, whatever we're doing, whoever we're with, the 'selfie' is the ultimate expression of who we are. This is me, it shouts, up close and personal. But who are we kidding? Isn't it all a big fat fantasy?

I know what you're thinking: what harm is there in the selfie? How can a little rectangular frame of our smiling face with a picturesque view behind it be a problem? Well, for me it is that background that is the problem. When we take a selfie we push ourselves to the front, block out whatever is behind, close our minds to others.

Visual detail makes abstract ideas come to life

Pattern of three strengthens argument

Use of analogy and ironic tone create a powerful sense of voice

The truth is that when we take selfies it's like we're seeking validation that our lives are important. More important than those of the people around us. Just imagine – you visit another country, another culture. There you are with your mates on the steps of a religious temple, or on a local beach with fishermen in the background, and all you can think of is yourself. The selfie reduces where we are, literally, to a backdrop – like a Hollywood set for our oh-so-important lives.

The other day, I left my mobile phone at home by mistake. Now, up until then I have been like everyone else, always snapping myself in places. Without my phone I got lost – and ended up walking down this back street on the way to school. For the first time, I looked properly at the houses – each one had a date above them. They were alms houses for the poor from the Victorian age. I know that because I looked it up – on my phone – when I got back! I'd never seen them before. I felt connected to the past.

Use of anecdote to support idea and change pace/tone of text

Short sentences convey idea of writer's change of heart

I suppose it's true that using selfies in moderation is fine. You could argue it's nice to have a snap of you and your Gran at her birthday tea. But – and this is the heart of the matter – there's something not quite right about us taking the snap of ourselves. We should be enjoying chatting to Gran, sharing a bit of cake. Let others snap us, if they want.

Counter argument fluently embedded and then answered by writer

Rhetorical questions evoke emotional response

There are far less harmful things in the world than selfies but they do represent something that's obsessive and narrow about the way we live. By making 'ourselves' the focus for attention, we begin to lose interest in others. Isn't it time we looked around and saw the lonely old man who'd like a chat, or explored the beautiful painting in the gallery rather than our face in front of it?

For 'selfie' read 'selfish'. I don't want to be like that.

Short paragraph 'rubber stamps' or concisely sums up argument as a whole

Comment

This is a very thoughtful, well-argued response which moves fluently from one idea to the next. It addresses all aspects of the task in depth and detail, and uses a wide range of language devices, manipulating them to make a powerful impact on the reader. The structure is balanced, and the argument sustained throughout – overall a convincing and highly effective blog.

5.4 Task C: Unseen poetry – analysing a writer's methods [pp. 72–73]

As you read the two responses below, bear in mind that the focus here is on how good expression can assist the response. The students' ideas would be assessed in the 'real' exam, but here we are focusing more on *how* these ideas are conveyed.

Sample A: Mid Level response

Opening paragraph providing a basic overview of poem

The poem is about the writer's memories of someone he loved and who loved him. He is remembering a time with her but by the end of the poem you realise a year has passed and they are no longer together.

Use of topic sentence to explain the poem's tone

Effective use of embedded quotations

To begin with the poem presents a happy, carefree picture. The poet says that the woman has 'bright hair flapping free' and this makes us think that everything is rosy in their relationship. The sound made is romantic and light with the alliteration – 'wandering, western sea.' In the second verse, the speaker even says they 'laughed light-heartedly', so it seems it was a happy, fun time.

Clear but simple explanation of language point

Interpretation weakened by poor expression

In the third verse, things start to go wrong. For example, suddenly it starts raining and the sea has a 'stain' on it. This isn't a good thing – it like hints at something spoilt or sad. But then the sun comes out and all is well for a moment.

Explanation of speaker's feelings is clumsily expressed

The fourth verse shows a change in time. The poet says the old cliff is still there and he asks the questions about whether he and the woman can go there again now that March has come around again. This is how you know it's been a year because he says 'that March' meaning the time at the beginning of the poem.

Language point is clear but sentence is rather awkward

The last verse reveals what has happened to them. The poet says that really it doesn't matter if the cliff is still there because he and his lover will go there 'nevermore.' It seems like she has forgotten or doesn't care about the place now, so it didn't mean as much to her.

Clear paragraph but with limited interpretation

Rhyme scheme not fluently linked to meaning

The rhyme scheme in the poem is one where each set of three lines has perfect rhymes but because the sounds aren't repeated in other verses it doesn't sound light-hearted or like a ballad. You don't really notice the rhyming much until the last word.

Overall, the poem is about how people don't judge situations properly or about how a memory can stick in your mind and mean more to you than others.

Overview offered in concluding paragraph not wholly relevant to task

Comment

The response is clearly organised with most paragraphs corresponding to the order of the verses. Points are usually clear and easy to understand and quotations are embedded effectively. Occasionally poor expression hinders deeper or more detailed exploration. The paragraph about rhyme is a bit out of place and the points made here would have been more effective if embedded in the other analysis.

Sample B: High Level response

Opening explanation goes straight to the heart of speaker's feelings	*The speaker's memories of 'Beeny Cliff' as the poem begins suggest a romantic, almost dream-like time, with the brilliant colours of 'opal' and 'sapphire' emphasising the precious nature of a past moment. This dream-like quality is emphasised by his companion 'riding high above' with her flowing locks – it as if she is a spirit of the sky, out of his reach.*

Additional clause adding interpretation to the main point

Use of structure fluently introduced	*Of course, it is not until the final verse that the reader learns of the separation of speaker and the woman. Whilst this could suggest the end of the relationship, the phrase 'nor knows of …' suggests that the lover is dead – because clearly she would know of the place, even if she didn't care about it. This adds poignancy to the beginning and makes the speaker's description of her understandable: he is romanticising and elevating her to something like a goddess.*

Possible interpretations explored though longer sentence

Analysis of language effects supported by embedded quotations	*The poem as a whole is really split into two halves and this helps the reader understand the speaker's reflections about the past and the present. The first three verses show the speaker dealing with memories – the use of the past tense 'loved' in the first verse, and time markers such as 'that clear-sunn'd day' reveal this is a past experience. The speaker uses the fourth verse to leap forward in time to the present as 'still….bulks old Beeny to the sky,' suggesting the unchanging natural world, before the final verse sees the poet stating that it is meaningless as the loved one is dead and can no longer enjoy it.*

Topic sentence signals switch to a new point	*The language elsewhere also helps the reader to trace the poet's feelings. Whilst there is life and energy early in the poem through the alliterative 'laughed light-heartedly' and onomatopoeic 'babbling' of the gulls, it is not long before the speaker talks of the 'little cloud' and the 'irised rain'. The change in the weather makes a 'dull, misfeatured stain' on the sea, as if the perfect picture is momentarily spoiled. The sun comes out again, but once we read the whole poem we can see this is a sort of omen.*

Use if appropriate language terms to explain ideas

Introduces key point at start of conclusion to draw ideas together	*Finally, it is important to note that the poet has named the poem 'Beeny Cliff'. He mentions its 'chasmal beauty' twice and also how it 'bulks old Beeny to the sky.' These references suggest that the cliff has an almost mythic quality, an ancient self that has seen lovers come and go. It will go on regardless of the pain and sufferings of mankind. So the poem is really about the speaker coming to terms with this reality. In using the word 'nevermore' to end the poem, he contrasts this blunt reality with the rhymed lyrical romance of the 'wild weird western shore' which his lover, in death, will never experience again.*

Complex sentence, punctuated effectively, links back to previous point

Comment

This is a detailed, fluent analysis that explains complex ideas coherently and thoughtfully. The paragraphs all have a specific focus but each contributes to an overall picture of the text. Quotations are carefully chosen and explored in depth through longer paragraphs or multi-clause sentences, without confusing the reader. Subject terminology is used accurately and contributes to the points made in the overall argument. This is an extremely effective and convincing analytical response.

GLOSSARY

active voice a form of the verb where the subject performs the action on the object of sentence. (e.g. 'The cat chased the ball of wool.') The active is more direct than the **passive voice**

adjective a word used to describe something or somebody (e.g. the *red* hat)

adverb a word used to modify a verb, adjective or another adverb, sometimes formed by adding 'ly' to an adjective (e.g. 'he spoke *nervously*')

alliteration where the same sound is repeated in a sequence of words, usually at the beginning of words

analogy an extended form of **metaphor** which creates a series of links between two different things

anecdote a short amusing or interesting story about a real incident or person

aside a remark or speech in a play that is intended to be heard only by the audience

assonance when the same sound appears in the same place in a series of words

audience the person or group of people who will read a text or watch a performance

ballad a traditional story written in rhyme

brackets a punctuation mark (()) used in pairs around extra information or around an afterthought in a sentence

caesura a pause during a line of poetry

chronological order the logical time order in which events take place

clause a phrase or group of words whose head is a verb. A clause can be a complete sentence

cliché a well-known descriptive phrase or expression that has lost impact through overuse (e.g. 'as right as rain', 'off like a shot')

climax the highpoint in the narrative arc of a play, act or story

cohesion how a text is structured so the individual parts (words, phrases, sentences or paragraphs) effectively create a single connected piece

colon a punctuation mark (:) that precedes a list, or when a character speaks in a play script or an expansion in a sentence

comedy a drama genre generally involving humour and usually a romance plot that ends happily

complex sentence a sentence with a main clause and one or more subordinate clauses (e.g. 'Although he liked to read, he rarely did.')

complication point in the **narrative arc** where the first problem or conflict arises, usually during the rising action stage of the plot

compound sentence a sentence with two equal clauses joined by and, 'or' 'but' or 'so' (e.g. 'The dog would sit but would not lie down.')

conditional clause A subordinate clause that lays out the conditions for something to happen, typically starting with the words 'if' or 'when' (e.g. 'If I get my homework done, I can relax in front of a film.')

conjunction a word that links two words or phrases together in a sentence to show the relationship between them

connective a general term for words or phrases which link sentences or parts of sentences, (e.g. 'and', 'while', 'furthermore', 'in the same way')

connotations meanings associated with a particular word, a thing or a concept (e.g. 'snow' = 'white', 'pure', 'cold')

consonance repeated consonant sounds within a sentence, paragraph or poem

contraction where a letter or letters in two words are omitted and replaced by an apostrophe (e.g. the contracted form of 'do not' is 'don't')

conventions language or structural features of a particular type of text

counter argument the opposite point of view from the one being taken in viewpoint speech or writing

dash a punctuation mark (—) used to separate a word or phrase from an independent clause

dependent clause see subordinate clause

dialogue speech and conversation between characters

enjambment in poetry when a line runs on into the next line without pause, so carrying the though with it. Sometimes called a run-on line

elegy a poem lamenting a death

ellipses a punctuation mark (...) that signals the omission of text or that more text should follow

explicit refers to information that is stated openly in a piece of writing

exposition the introduction of the setting, characters and situation early in the **narrative arc** in a story or a play

extended metaphor in poetry, a metaphor that continues some aspect of the image; it may continue into the next line or throughout the text

first person the narrative perspective that uses 'I'

flashback a scene or part of a play, novel or film that goes back in time, prior to the immediate action

flashforwards a scene or part of a play, novel or film that goes forward in time, beyond the immediate action

form a type of writing with particular features

formal a style used in most written professional language

fourth wall when the narrator or character in a novel or play addresses the audience directly. Originally, an imaginary wall on stage which faces the audience who are outside the action, which is broken

free verse a form of poetry; verses without regular rhythm or pattern, though they may contain some patterns, such as rhyme or repetition

genre a type of style of literary writing (e.g. a play, a novel, the Gothic, Fantasy writing, a ballad, a sonnet)

imagery descriptive language that uses word pictures to make actions, objects and characters more vivid in the reader's mind

implicit refers to information that is hinted at or suggested in a piece of writing

in media res when a story start in the middle of events

inference a meaning deduced from evidence in a text

informal a style used most in casual spoken language and some written texts

intensifiers words used to increase a sense of a writer's emotion or viewpoint, often adverb-adjective combinations (e.g. 'really awful weather' or 'utterly divine decoration')

irony deliberately saying one thing when you mean another, usually in a humorous, sarcastic or sometimes thoughtful way

lyric a poem, expressing the emotions and thoughts of the speaker but which usually explores a single feeling or idea

metaphor when one thing is used to describe another to create a striking or unusual image

metre the pattern of stressed and unstressed syllables in a line of verse

minor sentence a word, phrase, or clause which, while functioning as a sentence, lacks the grammatical completeness of a full sentence (e.g. 'Yes, indeed.' 'The more the merrier')

mood the tone or atmosphere created by an artistic work

mnemonic a memory aid that can, for example, help with remembering spelling

narrative arc the construction of the storyline in a novel or story from beginning through middle to end, though how it is told varies

narrator the voice or character that tells the story in a novel, narrative poem or play

naturalistic a style of drama and theatre that developed in the late 19th and early 20th centuries which attempts to create an illusion of reality through a range of theatrical strategies, such as staging and props

noun phrases a phrase with a noun at its head, often combining a noun and an adjective or adjectives, (e.g. 'noble loyalty', 'sumptuous banquet')

octave a verse of eight lines, usually in iambic pentameter, the first eight lines of a sonnet (where it is sometimes called two **quatrains**)

onomatopoeia a word that suggests its meaning through its sound (e.g. 'meow', 'squelch')

pace the speed or rate at which a text or a performance or a spoken text moves

paraphrase a rewording of something written or spoken

participle English verbs have two participles: present (e.g. 'talking') and past (e.g. 'talked')

passive voice a form of a verb in which the subject undergoes the action of the verb (e.g. 'They were greeted by an old man.' as opposed to the **active voice** 'An old man greeted them.')

personification the treatment or description of an object or idea as though they were human with human feelings and attributes

phrase a small group of words that work as a conceptual unit, typically a component of a **clause** (e.g. 'suggesting that she is')

plot the storyline of a novel, play or poem

preposition a word that shows the relationship of one thing to another (e.g. 'on' in 'the cloth lay on the table' or 'over' in 'the bird flew over the branch.')

prose the natural flow of speech used in novels and other works and unlike poetry which has a more emphasised rhythmic structure

protagonist the main or a major character

purpose the reason for or aim of writing a text

quatrain four lines of verse that can stand alone or be repeated

quotation words that are taken directly from a text or extract and which are signalled by the use of inverted commas around them

refrain repeated lines or groups of words that convey the same meaning

register the choice of language used appropriate to social class or the particular context

repetition repeated sounds, words or other uses of language

resolution the end of the **narrative arc** in a play or story where things are uncovered, explained or resolved

rhetorical question a question asked for effect rather than for an answer

rhyme scheme the pattern of rhyme in a poem

rhyming couplet a couplet (two paired lines) that rhymes

semicolon a punctuation mark (;) which is used to link two ideas, events or pieces of information

sentence types there are three main sentence types: the **simple sentence** – with one main clause consisting of subject and a verb; the **compound sentence** – with two equal clauses joined by 'and' 'or' 'but' or 'so'; the **complex sentence** – with a main clause and one or more subordinate clauses

simile when one thing is compared directly with another using 'like' or 'as'

simple sentence a sentence with one main clause consisting of subject and a verb, (e.g. The sun shone steadily.)

slang words and phrases that are regarded as very informal, are more common in speech than writing, and are typically linked to a particular context or group of people (e.g. snowboarders, police officers, older people)

soliloquy a dramatic technique that allows a character to speak as if thinking aloud, revealing their inner thoughts and intentions to the audience

sonnet a fourteen-line poem with a rhyming couplet at the end. Types of sonnet include the Shakespearian sonnet and the Petrarchan sonnet

stage craft the technical aspects of theatrical production, including stage management, constructing scenery, lighting design and procuring costumes and props

stage directions advice printed from time to time in the text of a play giving instructions or information to the actors, or on setting and special effects

Standard English the form of English most widely accepted as the conventional form

stanza a group or pattern of lines forming a verse

style the characteristics of a text that make it different from another

subordinate clause a clause that is secondary to another part of the sentence (e.g. 'I was late for the train, *even though I left early.*')

subordinating conjunction introduces a subordinate clause (e.g. 'while' in 'while I was waiting, ...')

symbol something that represents something else, usually with meanings that are widely known (e.g. a 'dove' as a symbol of peace)

synonym a word or phrase that is very similar in meaning to another (e.g. 'bitter' and 'acidic')

synthesising the process of taking information from one text and putting it together with information from another and drawing conclusions

tense the aspect of the verb that indicates the time at which an action takes place (e.g. present tense, past tense, future tense)

theme an idea running through a work of literature or art

third person the narrative perspective that uses 'he' or 'she'

tone see **mood**

topic sentence a sentence that expresses the main idea of a paragraph, sometimes the first of the paragraph

tragedy a drama genre usually involving the fall from high status or from grace of a noble but flawed character

voice the speaker or narrator of a poem or work of fiction. This persona is created in the speaker's mind, though sometimes it can seem close to the poet's or writer's own voice